W9-COU-821

ALL ABOUT BEGONIAS

ALL ABOUT BEGONIAS

Bernice Brilmayer

FOREWORD BY CLARENCE HALL

1960
DOUBLEDAY & COMPANY, INC.
GARDEN CITY, NEW YORK

*For my family—who have endured me, even encouraged
me, in this project from start to finish.*

Library of Congress Catalogue Card Number 60–11894
Copyright © 1960 by Bernice Brilmayer
All Rights Reserved
Printed in the United States of America
First Edition

FOREWORD

Of the many kinds of begonias, only two are widely known and grown: the showy summer-blooming tuberous, and the ever-blooming *semperflorens* cultivated in pots or garden beds. And people who know and grow one type are frequently unaware of the other.

This is a pity. Because, as the reader of this book will discover, there are many more varieties of begonias, each beautiful in its own right. In fact, the begonia family is so large and varied, it can be one of the most fascinating hobbies in floriculture. And it is a hobby that anyone can enjoy, whether he is limited to an indoor garden or blessed by climate that permits all-year outside growing.

The first function of this book, then, is to introduce you to the large family of begonias, with all its variations—to whet your appetite for more and more delightfully different types. You'll read about plants growing up to six feet tall, with great pendant clusters of pink, white, cream, red, rose, orange-colored flowers. You'll feast on the colors of the rex begonias' rich foliage. You'll discover some fascinating oddities; the trailers and climbers; the low-growing rhizomatous begonias that send up airy sprays of flowers in spring; the miniatures and giants.

Next, you'll find out how to grow them all—simple, nontechnical directions which are easy to understand and to follow: how to propagate begonias; how to create new varieties by hybridizing; how to use begonias decoratively in your home and garden. Here is the whole story of begonias, written clearly, readably, and with the warmth of someone who knows the plants well, and loves them.

This book is both inspiring and practical, of interest to neophyte, to plain dirt gardener, or to the one with the green thumb. It is an enthusiastic introduction to a royal hobby—knowing, growing, and enjoying begonias of all kinds.

CLARENCE HALL
National President
American Begonia Society

AUTHOR'S NOTE

When I fell in love with begonias, I had no idea that I was beginning this book. But as I grew them, people began to trust me with their questions about begonias; and I thought I saw a need for a book written specifically for amateurs, using the amateur's vocabulary, explaining how to make the most of average amateur growing conditions. I've made it as friendly and useful as I can.

Grateful thanks are due those who have helped me: Clarence Hall, President of the American Begonia Society; Elvin McDonald, my young horticultural mentor; Mrs. Leslie Daly, in whom friendship is unlimited; Mrs. Mary Ellen Ross; Mrs. Joy Logee Martin; Henry H. Teuscher; A. B. Graf; Ralph Bailey; R. B. Farnham, in particular; and many other wonderful people in general.

Contents

Illustrations

COLOR

BLACK AND WHITE

DRAWINGS *by the AUTHOR*

ALL ABOUT BEGONIAS

CHAPTER 1

Introduction to Begonias

Picture a plant hanging down the wall of a dark and barren Mexican cave. It is three inches high, with flat green leaves saw-toothed on the edge, and china-white flowers. It grows from a small, lima-bean-shaped tuber wedged in a soil-less chink between the rocks.

Or imagine looking up thirteen feet to the top of a Colombian plant to see showers of dainty white, fragrant flowers. Waving from a stem trunk ten inches in diameter are great lobed leaves measuring more than two feet any way, shining green on top and rusty-fuzzy beneath.

Now think of a bushy little window-sill plant with crisp, waxy foliage shining bronzy-red, and many-petaled, rich rose flowers as bouffant as a little girl's petticoat.

These plants are all begonias—in order of appearance, *cavum, parviflora,* and 'Bo Peep.' Each one is spectacularly different from the other, yet they all belong to one botanical family. Only their first name is the same.

There is no end to the variety in begonias. They have leaves the size of a penny or a palmetto; with colors—brilliant, subdued, metallic—from one end of the rainbow to the other; and textures from sheerest silk and velvet to moiré, tweed, velour, and puckered seersucker. Begonia flowers may have four petals or four dozen, in colors from heavenly white to fiery orange and red. Begonias can be climbers, creepers, trailers, pygmy bushes or stately trees.

There are miniatures like *ardicaulis,* with perky, pointed fresh green leaves no larger than your little fingernail; majestic giants like 'Ricky Minter,' dinner-plate leaves shimmering deep bronzy green, deeply waved and ruffled on the edge; antique Orientals like glowing, translucent *cathayana;* angel-wing begonias, dangling clusters of outsize flowers from the tips of bamboo-like stems; the royal kingdom of rex begonias—fluted, spiraled, pebbled, velvety foliage in all patterns and combinations of jewel-like hues.

Some begonias look so much like other plants that they seem to masquerade as the castor bean, palm, peach, elm, lettuce, pond lily, rose, fern. Some trailing begonias are so floriferous that their hanging baskets look ready to burst. There are begonias whose flowers grow beards, or whose leaves are upholstered in Gay Nineties plush; tuberous begonias, to glorify a summer garden bed or fill a window with bloom at Christmas; even individualists, which perform crazy capers, such as producing baby plants on the leaves at the top of the plant.

Even with this captivatingly wide variety, begonias are in general agreeable to growing in the home. They don't require the full sun of a southern exposure—frequently the only side of the house without a window suitable for growing plants. They need no hard-to-find potting mediums or fertilizers. They don't want to be continually pampered and hovered over. Given a minimum of your kind attention, begonias keep healthy and colorful, to decorate your home with living beauty. With a carefully selected small collection, you can have begonias in flower every month of the year.

Small wonder, then, that people want to know more about begonias. In planning a begonia book, the question is: Which people, and what do they want to know? Scientists and professional growers are interested in one type of botanical news and information. Home growers want something different and down to earth. It is for them that this book has been written.

ALL ABOUT BEGONIAS, then, makes no scientific pretense. Precise botanical terms, classifications, and history are bypassed in favor of the language of the amateur. Botanical descriptions are mentioned only when they may enhance the appeal of a begonia or speed up the "let's-get-acquainted" process. Begonias are grouped—and the groups are named—according to the way the home grower sees them, thinks of them, or speaks of them.

NOMENCLATURE

One "necessary nuisance" has been retained—accepted begonia nomenclature—although it is printed with some modification of top-level horticultural practice. The principles of nomenclature and typographical style are based on precedent established in many recognized horticultural books and periodicals.

The reader can single out natural species by the use of italics (*aridicaulis, manni*). Hybrids, chance seedlings, and the like can be spotted by the single quotation marks around the capitalized but nonitalicized names ('Ricky Minter'). To facilitate reading and conversational use of the names, the genetive *ii* ending is reduced to a single *i;* and the word *variety* or its abbreviation, *var.,* is omitted.

For spelling and information about the origin of begonias mentioned by name, the authority is the *Buxton Check List of Begonias.*

To the limit of one human's capacity, begonias are accurately named in this book. Whenever possible, tongue-twisting Latin words are translated, to make them more memorable. Nicknames and other popular appellations are included, in parentheses or otherwise; also notes on the origins of names, which bring them alive and make them meaningful.

Why is accurate nomenclature important? If your begonias are growing and giving you pleasure, does it matter what their proper names are? It does, if you want to communicate with other growers, or learn more about your plants from reference books, or avoid ordering duplicates from catalogues. Communication is also one reason why so many plant names are in Latin—the universal botanical language, understood and easily translated by amateurs and professionals of all nations.

Be prepared to find this matter of accurate names vexing at times. Everybody does. And the confusion stems from conditions which are entirely legitimate. For example, different growing conditions in different areas—or even on different window sills—can cause the color or habit of two plants of the same species to differ so drastically that they may seem like two different species. Yet it is the same plant in two different versions. Also, in the game of chance called hybridizing, two practically identical plants may appear at the same time in places thousands of miles apart. Each grower, not knowing of the other plant, christens his creation according to his own taste. This is one reason why the American Begonia Society's nomenclature functions are so complicated, but so important.

BEGONIAS DESCRIBED

More than six hundred begonias are described in these pages—actually, a "drop in the bucket" as far as this gigantic family of plants is concerned. But a book naming every begonia ever known would be utterly impossible to write and to carry around; and since many are not grown, and are not likely to be, half of it would be useless to most readers.

With the exception of a few obscure or not particularly outstanding plants, named begonias offered for sale—on-the-spot or by mail— are described in Chapters 6 through 15. When there are fairly distinct differences in availability and ease of culture, the varieties are subdivided under three headings:

> *For Beginners*—begonias which are widely available, and easiest of culture.
> *For Advanced Growers*—available begonias which require some special care and cultural know-how.
> *For Collectors*—begonias which are not available everywhere, but can be found; or which are the most finicky to grow; or both.

An additional, fourth classification—*Varieties to Watch or Wait for* —includes begonias which, to my best knowledge at the time this book goes to press, are not available for sale but are definitely worth having. This includes newly discovered species not yet ready for popular distribution, and numerous exciting new hybrids not yet disseminated. Undoubtedly, some of these will be on sale before this book is out of the printer's hands; and others may have been omitted because the news did not reach my ears or eyes in time to be included.

Now, here we go. Let's find out about begonias—how to know and grow them. This family of plants is so utterly fascinating and fabulous, you're being dared to discover just six varieties you never met before, and then to call it quits. You're challenged not to want—and continue to want—"just one more."

CHAPTER 2

What Is a Begonia?

How can you know whether a plant is a begonia, or something else? Not always by its name. The favorite old-time "strawberry begonia" (also called "strawberry geranium") which sends out runners with plantlets at the ends is actually a perennial, *Saxifraga sarmentosa.* The "watermelon begonia" is not a begonia, but a peperomia. The "begonia vine" is a cissus.

If a plant is a true begonia, you can identify it by certain characteristics of flower and foliage. All begonias do not have all these characteristics, but they do have a sufficient number to entitle them to membership in the begonia family of plants.

BEGONIA CHARACTERISTICS

Begonia flowers usually grow in branching clusters—not singly, like a daisy, one at the end of each stem. Each begonia flower is either male or female—not both, like the African violet, which has in one flower the reproductive organs of both sexes. A begonia bears separate male and female flowers on the same plant—not, like the holly, males on one plant and females on another.

It is easy to see the difference between the male and female begonia flowers. The male may have larger petals, but the female has a showy appendage—a three-winged, seed-bearing ovary immediately under the petals. A slice cut from this ovary when it contains ripe seeds is shaped like a Gothic church window.

Now, let's look at begonia leaves. They're usually lopsided; the portion on one side of the main vein is larger than the other. And they grow at alternate intervals out from the stem—not one opposite the other, but first to the right, next to the left, and on up the stem.

Most begonias have stipules—leaflike sheaths from which young leaves emerge—which are often transparent, may turn dry and papery with age. Some stipules remain for the life of the plant; some

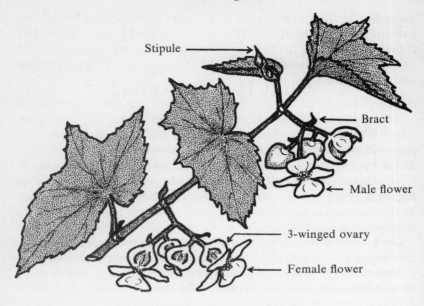

Stipule

Bract

Male flower

3-winged ovary

Female flower

TYPICAL BEGONIA CHARACTERISTICS

drop off. Some are hairy, some brightly colored, some inconspicuous green.

Begonia flowers usually have bracts—modified leaves which encase the buds, rather like the chaff of wheat. These are often colored the same as the flower petals.

No matter how small or large a plant, whether its habit is to creep or grow bushy, whatever the shape of its leaves or color of its flowers, if it is a begonia it will have some or all of these characteristics.

GROUPS OF BEGONIAS

It is extremely difficult, if not impossible, to classify begonias into neat, tidy groups. Usually, they're grouped by type of root—bulbous, tuberous, rhizomatous, fibrous. But this system is not clear cut. Rhizomatous begonias have fibrous roots, for example; a rhizome is not truly a root; many of the tuberous begonias are only partially so.

Over the years, begonia growers have evolved a kind of classification which seems to work well in everyday use. Plants are grouped according to their appearance or growing habit, with a fascinating catchall class for oddities that don't fit anywhere else. This system is helpful when you're selecting begonias to suit your personal taste or special growing conditions. It also permits the use of these familiar and descriptive titles:

Semperflorens (Wax) Begonias—"Ever-blooming" begonias with an abundance of waxy leaves and bountiful flowers off and on all year.

Angel-Wing Begonias—The term describes the shape of the leaf.

Hairy-Leaved Begonias—The foliage is velvety or whiskery.

Other Upright and Branching Begonias—Those which don't easily fit into the first three groups.

Basket Begonias—Their trailing or hanging habit makes them effective in hanging baskets.

Rhizomatous Begonias—Those which grow from a rhizome, a thickened, scarred stem which creeps over the ground, or ascends.

Rex Begonias—Famed for their brilliantly colored and exotically patterned foliage.

Winter-Blooming Tuberous Begonias—Floriferous florists' and greenhouse plants, more or less dormant in summer.

Summer-Blooming Tuberous Begonias—Glorious flowering plants for the semishaded garden, dormant in winter.

Odd and Rare Begonias—Offbeat or exotic varieties for collectors and others who favor the unusual.

Inevitably, this system—or any other I've seen—is plagued by overlapping. Some hairy leaves are shaped like an angel's wing. Rex begonias are also rhizomatous. There are some semituberous begonias which do not go dormant at any time of year, but too few to warrant giving them a group of their own.

In the following chapters, begonias are grouped according to what seem to be their most prominent features—admittedly a matter of personal opinion and judgment. If you can't locate a variety in the class to which you think it should belong, the index by varieties may be helpful.

Each of these begonia groups will enjoy a chapter of its own, with specific cultural and propagating notes where the practices vary from the general principles in Chapter 3, plus illustrations and descriptions of available varieties, and of others worth hunting for.

How To Grow Begonias

To the request for clear-cut, hard-and-fast rules for growing begonias —or any plants, for that matter—the most accurate answer is that there aren't any. True, there are some basic principles which, if carefully salted with care and common sense, will help create growing conditions to please the taste of most begonias. But this is a large and varied family of plants, originating in many and varied lands. Also, the growing conditions in your area may be entirely different from those in mine. And successful growing in your house may differ drastically even from the house of your green-thumb neighbor next door.

On second thought, there is one sound and sensible rule: watch your plants intelligently. Like babies, begonias don't talk; but they can kick up quite a fuss if they're neglected, mistreated, or ill. Sometimes, simply moving a plant to a different window will give it a new lease on life. Or watering a little more, or a lot less. Or merely cleaning off city soot and dust from the leaves.

Which leads us to another golden rule. If your plants are growing well, don't change your methods on anybody's say-so—certainly not mine—without first making sure that the change is applicable to your own plants and growing environment. Even then, make the change tentatively, slowly, for only a few plants at a time.

Consider all the varying parts of the world where Nature planted begonias—teeming, steaming jungles; high and low altitudes; mossy, moist forests; cool, foggy cliffs and mountains; in acid leaf mold and near limestone rock. Now think of the extremes and in-betweens of climate on our continent—the differences in intensity and hours of sun and light; the many kinds of soil, from Georgia clay to Florida sand. So many elements complicate the cultural picture that what is sure-fire for one grower may very likely be sure death for another.

Right here—and again later—a word to the wise about winter. Even for humans, these are dark, dull, uninspiring days. For many house plants of all kinds, this is a time of rest. This resting period, or dormancy, is prevalent in some groups of begonias, affects isolated varieties in other groups. Sadly, some growers are frightened when a previously healthy plant suddenly drops its leaves, slows up, or stops growing—and the discouraging plant is discarded, pot and all. When a plant shows signs that it wants to rest in winter, let it. Give it less water—and no fertilizer—and it will often pop up again with new growth in earliest spring.

Rex 'Can-Can' is not dying—just going dormant.

One more note—to straddle the two sides of a debate. Is it better to let begonias grow as large and lush as they will, regardless of age, or frequently to start fresh with newly rooted cuttings and relegate the old roots to the compost? The plants themselves can answer this. If they grow big and beautiful, and you like them that way, let them go at least until they outgrow your largest pots. But if they grow awkward and ungainly, or if your growing space is limited, then younger, smaller plants are more suitable.

Except for some delicate collectors' items, begonias are culturally adaptable and willing. They respond beautifully to intelligent care. They don't want or need to be hovered over or pampered, or to be a worrisome burden. Again like babies, they'll cheerfully accept more neglect and abuse than we dare to realize. When something goes temporarily wrong, they're amazingly quick to recover.

Good growing companions for begonias, in the same environment, are African violets, episcias, and gloxinias. Many a dyed-in-the-wool fancier of these and other members of the gesneriad family has tried one or two begonias, and wound up with two collecting interests— and vice versa.

The following cultural suggestions should be accepted as a general rule, and should be adapted two ways—to suit you, your home or greenhouse, and your resources; and to suit different types of plants. In each group of begonias there are some idiosyncracies which are noted and prescribed for in Chapters 6 through 15. Where an individual variety has an even more specific cultural peculiarity, it is noted with the varietal description.

TEMPERATURE

The easy-to-live-with begonia clan will be happy, in general, in temperatures ranging from 65° at night to 70°–75° by day—with some give and take at either end of the scale. Since stronger growth usually results from cooler temperatures, you may want to emulate one grower who wears a sweater indoors in winter, so her plants can keep cooler. But this is by no means necessary. This temperature, by the way, should be measured in the area where the plants actually grow—not in some warmer, remote corner of the room.

LIGHT

Although begonias are often called "shade plants," they seldom thrive and rarely bloom in shade. Yet the misnomer has led many people to try to grow them in dark places, such as the top of a coffee table, some distance from a source of daylight.

The process by which plants manufacture food (photosynthesis) is triggered by light. Try this demonstration. Stick a small piece of paper over one half of a leaf, and see how that half turns from healthy green to sickly yellow. If you can't read a telephone directory in the light where your begonias grow, there is not enough light. When light is inadequate, a plant stretches and strains toward whatever glimmer it can find, growing leggy, lanky, and ugly in the process.

Sunlight is another matter. Except in southern areas, begonias need as much sun as you can give them during the fall and winter months —from October through February in most regions. Where sunlight is especially sparse in winter, it's helpful to place plants under a reading lamp for several hours after twilight every day.

In summer, the hot noonday sun will scorch most begonias. Early-morning and late-afternoon sun is more to their liking.

Which window exposure provides the best begonia light? It depends on your house, your plant, and the season of the year. A good general rule is: south in winter, east in summer. Not, of course, if your south window is ten feet away from—and shaded by—the house next door, or if a stately old elm shelters you darkly on the east.

Here's an easy test of good begonia light. Take similar cuttings from one plant; root and pot them; and try one in each window where you might grow plants. The plant with the most bushy, compact growth and willing bloom will be in the happiest location. The specimen with long, straggly stems that lean and topple in one direction is in need of more light.

HUMIDITY

This is a two-dollar word for "moisture in the air." It is important to the health of human beings and plants. In summer, when windows are wide open and plants are out-of-doors, the air has more moisture than when furnace-heated in winter. Except in desert areas or during droughts, you can see the result in lush growth. Begonias which continually drop their leaves and keep forming new ones, or which have crisp, dried leaf edges, are usually in need of more humidity.

There are several ways you can help humidify the air around your plants. Grouping a number of pots in one growing area is one. Another is misting with a fine water spray daily, twice daily, or even thrice daily, depending on how dry the air is. You can use an emptied window cleaner bottle, or one of the devices sold for the purpose.

Effective, if sufficiently frequent, is dunking a plant—upside down, leaves and all—in a pan of water. This also cleans dust from the pores of the leaves, so they breathe and feed more easily. Foliage should not be wet, however, when the sun is shining on it, or at night.

Humidifying trays will cost you some extra initial effort and expense, but will pay off in many ways. They may be tailor-made (watertight, of course) in any size or shape—preferably at least two inches deep—to fit window sills, shelves, or other growing areas. A temporary tray shaped from a double thickness of heavyweight aluminum foil, and filled with some light material like vermiculite, will serve for months at low cost. For a larger investment in made-to-order trays of galvanized iron, you can have a more permanent asset (which can be prettily painted) that will hold heavier material like gravel or sand. The layer of vermiculite, gravel, sand, or what-have-you is kept constantly wet almost up to the bottom of the pot. Pots are set *on,* not *in,* the moist material.

From these trays, moisture is constantly evaporating—and humidifying—the air around the plant above.

Even though humid, indoor air should also be fresh—not stale or "close." Opening a window or door, where it won't give plants chilblains from icy drafts, is good daily practice.

WATER

So many plants are killed by the kindness of overwatering! Of all the begonias lost, the greatest number succumb to wet feet. Too much water causes the roots to rot; and there's no cure for it. But too little water can usually be remedied by thoroughly soaking pot and soil. Limp, wilted leaves and stems will spruce up surprisingly in a short time.

How often should plants be watered? Not every day, every other day, once a week—or on any other regular schedule—but when they need it. The size of pot, where it's placed, the soil inside it—even the weather outdoors—influence frequency of watering.

How can you tell when a plant needs water? Most infallibly, by feeling the soil with your fingers. If it's moist and sticks to your skin, don't water. If it's dry and crumbly, do—and water thoroughly, so the whole ball of soil is wet and the excess drains out the hole in the bottom of the pot. You can also test by tapping the side of a clay pot—a hollow ring is a signal to water. Or, dry pots and soil weigh less than moist ones.

Here are some variations on the watering theme:

Water more often . . .	*Water less often . . .*
Warm temperatures.	Cool (65° or less).
Air very dry.	Air humid.
Weather bright, sunny.	Cloudy, rain, or snow.
Plant growing actively.	Plant resting, or dormant.
Soil light, airy, porous.	Heavy soil.
Stems fibrous, woody.	Stems juicy, succulent.
Leaves large or thin.	Leaves small or thick.

At any time—and especially when the air is cool—cold water can shock a plant like an icy shower. Let faucet water stand until it reaches room temperature. Or if you're in a hurry, simply raise the temperature by adding warm water.

What kind of water? This is not a silly question. Neither is the average water in today's homes a serious plant problem. But if your water is near either extreme of the hard-soft scale, it may contain minerals begonias don't care for. Artificially softened water is also suspect. Rain water is above reproach, except in large cities or near factories, where it absorbs toxic gasses from the air on its way down.

POTTING SOIL MIX

Prescribing a precise recipe for begonia potting soil is plagued by more problems than you can shake a stick at. The ingredients are different in different parts of the country. Different environments call for different types of potting mix; and so do different begonias.

If your present potting soil is giving good results, you're taking a chance to change it, no matter what you hear or read about some magic new formula. On the other hand, improper soil is a fairly frequent cause of trouble.

Generally, a good begonia soil mix:

Should . . .	*Should not . . .*
Feel light, porous.	Pack down heavily.
Hold some moisture, but let excess water drain through.	Stay muddy after watering, or dry out immediately.
Look loose and airy at top of pot.	Form a hard surface crust.
Test slightly acid, or neutral.	Test extremely acid, or alkaline.
Supply a minimum of plant food.	Be overrich in fertilizer.

In making the ideal begonia soil, you have three basic ingredients to work with—soil, some kind of humus-y organic matter, and sand or some other coarse, inert material. Ideally, the good mix starts with equal proportions of these ingredients, but only as a point of departure. The proportions vary according to such factors as soil sandiness, humus content, and the like. Start, then, with one-third soil, one-third humus, and one-third sand—but:

If your potting soil is	*Add:*
Claylike; packs down and stays packed	more humus.
Soggy; water won't drain through	more sand.
Sandy; water runs right past the roots	no sand; more humus.
Spongy; has no "substance"	less humus; more soil containing clay.

Each of the three basic ingredients also comes in various forms, with varying characteristics which affect the final mix.

Soil

Here, texture is extremely important. If the soil from your yard is light and airy, a happy medium between clay and sand, you're blessed. As a test, rub a pinch of dirt between thumb and forefinger, then drop it. See how many fine particles remain sticking to your fingers. The "dirtier" your fingers, the more clay and silt your soil contains. (Silt is the soil texture midway between sand and clay.) If the dirt feels raspy when fingers are rubbed together, it is high in sand content; if it feels silky, it has more clay.

You can test soil for acidity or alkalinity with litmus paper from the drugstore. A piece is inserted in moist soil, or—for a clearer color picture—in water in which soil has been allowed to settle. When pink litmus paper turns blue, it indicates alkalinity. Blue litmus paper turning strong pink in a hurry signals fairly strong acidity; if it slowly turns soft pink, it may be slightly acid, just about right for most begonias.

The litmus test does not give calibrated degrees of acidity or alkalinity, as would the use of the fresh soil-reaction liquid in a "soil test kit." It will, however, tell you whether your soil is so alkaline that, for begonias, extra quantities of acid-making peat or other humus should be added. And it will serve as a stand-in while you send a soil sample to your county agricultural agent for more specific recommendations.

Humus

In general, this term describes any decayed vegetable, or organic matter which is in soil or added to it. It may mean leaf mold, peat, rotted tree trunks, compost, or all these lumped together.

Peat moss is decayed sphagnum moss dug from bogs, and is available in both coarse and powdery forms. Peat (without "moss") is usually a younger, less durable material. Manures—well rotted or dehydrated—provide a form of humus. Compost is, of course, vegetable matter you pile up in your yard which, when properly decayed, is humus.

In the woods, humus is the third layer of debris under trees—and if you live near a supply of it, you are rich indeed. On top are the loose, dry, undecayed leaves. Immediately under these is the leaf mold—pieces of leaves, bark, and twigs in various stages of decomposition. The third layer is humus—leaf mold which has been more completely decomposed. It is usually dark brown or black, and is worth its weight in gold when scraped up, carried home, sifted through a half-inch screen, and added to a soil mix.

Generally or specifically, humus is not strictly a plant food. Its purpose is to improve soil structure, to help hold and store food in the soil and make it more readily available. Humus in a soil mix lightens its texture, makes it more mellow, encourages strong root growth. Humus helps soil hold water—valuable where there are dry, hot summer winds.

On the other hand, humus should not be used with reckless abandon. Too much humus keeps soil too moist, causes root rot, and encourages mildew. Dry, insufficiently decomposed humus material is too busy completing the decomposition process to perform its proper functions. Some pieces of leaves and twigs left in the mix help create drainage channels, but too much is too much. Humus packed tightly into a pot holds water like a sponge. When humus is stored in a warm place for months on end, it can build up too much nitrogen for good root growth.

Sand

The purpose of sand in a soil mix is to speed drainage. But so much depends upon what kind of sand it is—obviously, not the fine white seashore brand. Specifications usually call for "sharp" or "builder's" sand, with larger particles which permit air to reach roots, and water to drain through. You can beg a bucketful of builder's sand at the site of a construction project—it's used in mixing cement or mortar. You can buy it too, but not usually in small quantities. Or your builders' supply house may have pea-sized gravel, an excellent substitute when used in smaller proportions than sharp sand.

Another sand substitute is bird gravel, available at most variety or pet stores. Other materials offered for aerating soil and promoting good drainage are: vermiculite, several brands of pelletized volcanic rock, finely shredded redwood. All these have the capacity to take in and hold moisture, which is not true of sand. Consequently, a mix containing any of these substitutes would be watered with a restrained hand.

Fertilizers

Until or unless you're sure of yourself, it's a good idea to omit fertilizers from a potting soil mixture. There will be natural sustenance to maintain the plant while its roots are settling themselves in new quarters. After that, you can supply fertilizer (see *Fertilizing* page 34) when the plant needs extra food. However, many growers mix in bone meal, superphosphate, and/or balanced chemical fertilizers with discretion, and in limited amounts. These mixes benefit by sitting and "seasoning" for a few weeks before use.

For sizable plant collections, mixtures of potting soil are conveniently made in large batches—in buckets or even galvanized garbage cans. Ingredients are mixed thoroughly and with little effort by putting the top on the can, and rolling or tumbling it for a while. Smaller quantities are easily mixed in an empty bag—paper, plastic, or even a fertilizer bag. Hold the top closed with one hand, grab the bottom with the other, and shake or turn upside down and back again. Potting soil should always be moist when it is used.

Sterilizing soil discourages insects and disease. Use commercial chemicals for the purpose carefully, and according to directions. Or oven-bake a small quantity of moist soil in a covered container, with the heat adjusted to low (about 200°), until the center of the soil reaches oven temperature. Or get 40 per cent commercial formaldehyde at your drugstore. Mix a quarter of a teaspoon with five cups of moist soil and let stand, covered, for twenty-four hours. Uncover, stir, and set aside until the fragrance departs.

For a limited number of plants—or the plenteous purse—ready-mixed soils are available at garden supply houses and variety stores. For begonias, the "general-house-plant" mix is usually more suitable than either cactus or African-violet soil. It should be used fresh, not stored for long periods.

Also available are trade-named soil substitutes which work well when package directions are followed carefully. Usually these require moistening before use, and more fertilizing and watering in use than a regular soil mix.

Recent experiments in growing begonias in nonnutritive mediums such as sphagnum moss have produced excellent results—particularly with some of the more finicky varieties, or in hot and humid climates. Since sphagnum is absorptive and holds moisture for some time, watering must be carefully controlled. Fertilizer, which should be "balanced" with necessary plant food elements, is supplied on a regular schedule. Many rare and beautiful begonias at the Montreal Botanical Gardens grow in sphagnum. If you want to try the method, be sure you get the latest accurate information from some reliable source.

POTTING

Unlike the deep-digging carrot or Oriental poppy, begonias are naturally shallow-growers; their roots stay fairly close to the soil surface. With few exceptions, shallow pots—bulb, azalea, or African-violet pans—are most suitable. Whether you choose porous clay pots or lightweight plastic pots depends upon growing conditions and personal preference. In behalf of clay, there is porosity which permits air to enter and escape from the soil inside the pot, and water to evaporate. Plastic pots hold moisture longer, may be tricky if you have a heavy hand with the watering can, but are easier to keep clean and to handle.

In repotting, the new pot should be only one size larger than previously, and not much deeper than before. Pots should be scrubbed thoroughly clean; clay pots may be sterilized by boiling. Package-recommended solutions of chlorine laundry bleach or Lysol will also sterilize pots soaked in them for some days. Since dry clay pots may soak up moisture needed by the plant as it re-establishes itself, they are more safely soaked in water before use.

When do begonias need repotting? If you have a large collection, you can indulge in one convenient potting spree, spring and fall, for all plants. However, if individual plants can be given a choice, you'll repot when they ask for it. When you see roots growing out of the drainage hole in the bottom of the pot; when a plant is mysteriously standing still at a time when it should be growing actively, holding its own but not growing; when you tap the soil ball gently out of the pot into your hand and see that it is tightly bound by a solid mass of rootlets—these are go-ahead signals for a larger pot and some fresh new soil. When plants first arrive in your home from a friend, greenhouse, or florist, whether or not they seem to be in need of potting, it's often safer to allow them a few weeks to adjust to the new environment first.

There are pros and cons about whether begonias prefer to be pot-bound or pot-loose. Some say a plant with its roots cramped in a tight pot—and this may be particularly true of types like the wax begonias—will flower more profusely. Some say an uncrowded pot encourages more luxuriant foliage.

The likely truth is (and this may sound like the second verse of the same song), it depends upon the type of plant and upon cultural conditions such as moisture and humidity. Pot-bound plants must obviously be fertilized regularly. Overpotted plants should not be overwatered, or the roots can smother. One indisputable fact is that a small plant—a seedling or a newly rooted cutting, without a full root system—will die a quick death in a pot several sizes too large.

In repotting a pot-bound begonia, first break the root ball gently in a few places to encourage young roots to reach out to the new soil. Place a drainage layer of pebbles or broken crock in the bottom of the new pot, and hold the plant in the center so that the crown (the central spot where stems join to meet roots) is a half-inch below the rim of the pot. Fill the sides with new soil and press down lightly— on the sides only—leaving the top half-inch empty, to make watering easier. Begonias should not be packed too firmly. Water thoroughly, and set the plant in a protected spot until it recovers from the shock of the move.

FERTILIZING

Once again, moderation is the rule. Overanxious, heavy-handed fertilizing can cause as many woes as overwatering. Authorities say that plants need much less nutrition than we think.

When should a begonia be fed? Not when it has just been repotted; not when it is dormant; not when it is weak and ailing; not immediately after its flowering period. Fertilize when a plant begins to produce new growth after a resting period, or about six weeks to two months before its normal flowering period, and until flowering is finished.

There are many kinds of suitable fertilizers, each with its own advantages to offer. In addition to humus and soil-conditioning properties, well rotted manure (not fresh)—if you can get it—supplies natural food value. Dehydrated manures make the same contributions, but in smaller proportions. Weak manure "tea," made by steeping well-rotted manure tied in a square of burlap in water for a week or so, provides food so quickly available that plants sometimes seem to make new growth almost before your eyes. This "forced feeding" will sometimes help hurry a plant into shape for a show, but should not be a frequent or regular practice.

There are a number of convenient, soluble plant foods which are easily applied at watering time—but never when the soil is completely dry. Recommended solutions spelled out in package directions should be followed carefully.

Fish meal or emulsion is also excellent for begonias—but cats love it too, sometimes with harrying effects on the plants.

Vitamin B_1 can be fed to plants—not as a fertilizer, but to promote stronger root systems. Household ammonia supplies a small amount of nitrogen, but if it contains soap, it may make the soil sticky. Several other materials around the house can, and have been used successfully on plants; but unless you know your soil—and your chemistry—you're safer to stick with products specially for the purpose.

Some ten or more years ago the practice of foliar feeding—applying food to plant leaves—became popular, particularly for forcing plants into fast growth for exhibiting in competition. It is a fact that leaves can absorb food through the pores and send it down to growing plant parts. Nearly all soluble nutrients may be fed this way, and will be absorbed through both sides of the leaf. Recommended for foliar feeding is a half-strength fertilizer solution, applied in a spray or mist, every two weeks for a month or more. It should never completely replace root feeding.

GROOMING

Whether or not your plants are frequently "at home" to visiting plant lovers, year-round good grooming is sound practice because it promotes good health. This includes beauty-parlor service on a regular schedule—at least once a week—but it need not be tedious or involved.

Some good-grooming practices seem obvious, but are often overlooked. Dead or dying flowers and leaves should be cut off cleanly. Leaves can't breathe unless they're clean. They can be dusted with a tissue—or the whole plant may be dipped into a sink or pail of clean, warm water. Tip growth should often be pinched out, to encourage branching and bushy shape. Begonias which tend to grow tall need staking; and growing shoots should be frequently retied to a stake.

Window-sill plants should be turned regularly—at least twice a week—so they don't lean drunkenly toward the light. When the soil surface is hard and caked, it should be scratched loose; when it's covered with accumulated white fertilizer salts or green, mosslike algae, it should be scraped clean and replaced with fresh soil.

Middle-aged plants sometimes grow straggly and need fairly severe pruning. When new growth begins in early spring, cutting out older wood gives new shoots a better chance to develop.

Well-gromed plants are well grown—and the reverse. This is often what makes a "green thumb" green.

SUMMERING BEGONIAS OUT-OF-DOORS

When your plants spend their summer vacation outside, they're usually happier—and so are you. Nature will do some watering for you, with pure rain. Plants will grow fuller, more compact with overhead sky light; flower and foliage colors are fresher and richer.

Begonias spend the summer out-of-doors,
their pots sunk to the rim in soil.

Usually, you're safe to set house plants out-of-doors three weeks after the average date of the last frost in your locality.

Summer quarters can be simple or elaborate, makeshift or decorative, temporary or permanent. You can set a single begonia in the light sun beside your front door; or arrange pots on benches or shelves, in window boxes or planters, on tables or special stands; or shelter them in a lath house; or arrange them to colorful advantage in the light shade and protection of a wall or hedge, or in the dappled sun under a tall tree.

Pots may be sunk up to the rim in soil. A layer of cinders in the bottom of the hole discourages earthworms from entering the pots. A ring of lime around the pot, or a pile of slug bait, will ward off snails and slugs with a notoriously voracious appetite for tender, juicy begonia leaves. Mulching with a two-inch layer of peat moss or buckwheat hulls will cut down weeding and watering.

In hot, dry weather, begonias appreciate frequent fine misting with the hose. In areas where hot, dry winds blow for days on end, extra humidifying devices should be rigged up. Wetting down walks, lawn, and other surrounding areas will help—or stretching a screen of damp burlap around two sides of the plant area, or a sheet hung between begonias and house or wall and kept damp. In extreme situations, precious begonias have been known to spend these torrid summer days in cooler, damp cellars.

Don't set begonias where they can be damaged by strong wind- and rainstorms—or where they can be scorched by strong sun. Early-morning and late-afternoon sunlight encourages good coloring and flowers. Hot noon sun discolors leaves and flowers and dries leaf edges. Dark, unbroken shade produces lanky, unhealthy growth.

A temporary lath shelter or a well-designed lath house is a comfortable asset. It provides cooler temperatures, higher humidity, and protection from heavy winds and rain. Laths are generally spaced the width of a lath apart, to provide 50 per cent shade; slanted so that rain will run off, not drip down on, plants; and run north and south, so shade inside moves with the sun. A coat of white paint deflects more light.

In the fall, bring begonias back indoors ten days to two weeks before windows will be closed and the heat turned on, so they can adjust gradually to drier indoor air.

BEGONIAS IN THE HOME GREENHOUSE

Although a greenhouse is by no means necessary, it does facilitate growing some of the more rare and exotic begonias. And, of course, all varieties will thrive in these near-ideal conditions. Culture is generally the same as for house-grown plants, with some slight variations.

Greenhouse potting soil is usually somewhat heavier than the standard mixture. Humidity is more easily maintained than in the home. Shading from hot sun may begin as early as March and continue through October. Rex begonias are often grown in shade under benches, sometimes with added light from fluorescent fixtures.

During protracted humid and rainy seasons, begonias are kept as dry as possible, with the best possible air circulation. Overcrowding on benches is dangerous. At least one commercial grower has installed a fan and an air dryer for these difficult periods when rot can run rampant. Others grow begonias on specially spaced, elevated steps, in preference to flat benches, to facilitate air circulation. Doors and ventilators are kept wide open in summer heat and humidity. Tight screening helps keep plants insect- and disease-free.

GROWING BEGONIAS UNDER ARTIFICIAL LIGHT

Since the fairly new—and so exciting—discovery that plants can and will germinate, propagate, flower, and mature without ever seeing the light of day, many a cellar workshop has given way to an

Rex begonias grow well in cellar under fluorescent lights.

indoor greenhouse. This has been a blessing to hobbyists with a yen for green-growing things, but without space or resources to indulge the passion; to growers who work by day and enjoy working with their plants in the evenings; even to greenhouse owners, who are frustrated by winter's long, dark nights and short days—and also by the obiquitous problem of a shortage of space.

Right here, an important point should be made clear. Growing plants under artificial light is still a mysterious, new, uncompleted experiment. There is no "last word" on the subject. Science has established many facts, but more are still to be explored and proved. The following is simply a report on some growers' experiences with fluorescent lighting (including my own) and does not pretend to be scientifically authentic or complete.

Because begonias do not require full sun—which artificial lighting has not yet duplicated—they are good subjects for growing under fluorescent lights. Here again, they are akin to African violets in cultural needs. The rex begonias are probably the most satisfactory type for growing this new way. Wax begonias and angel-wings would require the most intense light of all groups.

In the dark, short days of winter, many begonia varieties will pass up the usual yearly dormancy when they receive light from a mechanical source—a living-room lamp, or a desk or kitchen fluorescent fixture—for three or four hours after sundown. This extra light ration will also bring many out of dormancy ahead of schedule. And it will help maintain health and growth in other varieties which merely take life easy for a while in winter.

At the other extreme are hundreds of cellars, in all parts of the country, which gleam with light-reflecting pure white paint and are crammed with plant-filled shelves stacked up like bunk beds. Midway are the dark closets and cupboards now bright with fluorescent light and green with growing plants; the formerly shady north windows now, with added light, growing beautiful begonias.

Some tests indicate that seeds germinate faster and more perfectly, seedlings develop faster and more uniformly, under these controlled lighting conditions. Amazing experiments have reported superfast rooting of cuttings. Summer-blooming garden tuberous begonias now force easily into winter bloom. Here is a fabulous new way to grow plants!

Good results with artificial light are naturally based on all the elements of good culture. Proper temperature, humidity, soil mix, and other factors are equally important, no matter where a plant is placed to grow; and the requirements here are much the same as for ordinary house or greenhouse growing.

Types of Fluorescent Tubes

Opinions vary here. One authority maintains that daylight tubes should be used for flower production; cool white tubes for rooting and root growth. Another believes that the type of tube is not nearly so important as the intensity of light—witness the obvious spurt of growth when old, faded tubes are replaced with new. Until some scientific rule is laid down for begonias, the tubes might well be mixed—one or more of each type.

Some reports have recommended the addition of incandescent light, to supply "red rays of the sun" and promote bloom, but this is still a controversial principle. Many begonias have bloomed beautifully under fluorescent tubes alone. Incandescent bulbs should be used with care, since they generate heat which can burn plants and may dangerously lower humidity.

Light Intensity

Proper light is created by placing the plants at the correct distance from the tubes—and maintained by renewing the tubes at minimum six-month intervals. An estimated 25 per cent of light can be lost in the first four to six months of use.

Mathematically, light intensity decreases in proportion to distance of lamp from plants. At six inches, for example, the light is approximately four times stronger than at twelve inches. Flat plants like African violets are fortunate: a light from eight inches above their heads has no great distance to travel—and intensity to lose—before it touches the soil. Begonias, of more varying heights, are at a disadvantage, but they can be accommodated. Lights are placed eight inches above the tops of taller varieties, and shorter plants are set up on inverted pots or special stands. Eventually the taller plants will grow until they touch the tubes. Rather than raising the fluorescent fixture, it is better to snip out the top of the plant. It will quickly grow bushy and be attractive again. By rooting the cut portions, you'll have extra plants to share with friends and neighbors.

Incidentally, artificial light need not be as intense as outdoor light is at noon, because daylight waxes and wanes, while fluorescents burn steadily.

With good cultural conditions, many begonias will bloom bountifully under four forty-eight-inch-long, 40-watt tubes in industrial type fixtures with fifteen-inch reflectors. This setup will adequately light a bench or table twenty-four to thirty inches wide. To Bruce Thompson, whose cellar is an immaculate and precisely managed greenhouse, is due credit for year-round performance proof of these figures, and many other facts in this summary of fluorescent-light gardening. His specimen gloxinias have copped many flower-show prizes, but they never see the sunlight until they're taken to be displayed.

Timing

Begonia lights should burn constantly for fourteen to sixteen hours a day. An automatic timer will turn lights on and off—or you can flick the switch yourself.

And here's a fascinating fact. During plants' eight hours of dark and rest, turning on the lights—even for a few minutes—will interrupt the growth cycle. Perhaps the plants think it's another new day? At any rate, some flowering types—like tuberous begonias—have been forced into bloom faster with the use of intermittent short periods of light. But here again, facts are often few and unproved. Unless you're an expert, or born daring, the consistent fourteen to sixteen hours of light followed by eight to ten hours of rest is recommended.

Cost

Most growers have started with one limited fluorescent-lighted growing area; but few have stopped there. Once you've set up your second set of fixtures, you've probably passed the minimum watt usage for household purposes, and the rate scale becomes cheaper, the more kilowatt-hours of electricity you use. Depending on rates in your area, one fixture with four 40-watt tubes will operate for approximately six cents a day.

Results

Most begonias grown under adequate fluorescent lighting have proved, to my satisfaction at least, as healthy, sturdy, and floriferous as the same varieties, window sill-grown in winter. And many growers with limited resources or facilities have been able to join the begonia fan club—and even to outstrip other growers with some of the more touchy varieties. There's one wonderful comfort in this kind of growing—the weather makes little or no difference in results; there are no dark days, no weeks of continual rain, no sizzling noon sun. The light can be kept constant, and other cultural conditions can be controlled.

This report on artificial lighting may be recklessly enthusiastic. But it has worked—for so many plants, and for so many amateur growers. If you ever wanted to know and grow begonias, here is your wide-open welcome. If you have a closet which can be emptied, a bookcase, cupboard, dark window, or cellar—now you can let yourself go and grow every begonia for which you can find a spot to set the pot.

GEOGRAPHICAL VARIATIONS IN BEGONIA GROWING

Some parts of our country have the most suitable soil for growing begonias; others have such ideal climate, many varieties can be garden-grown the year round. In some areas, growing begonias can be almost too easy to be interesting; in others, it's a constant challenge. But nobody has all the luck. And there is no place where begonias cannot be grown. Here are some suggestions, general and specific, for making the best—or the most—of what the weatherman deals out, wherever you may be.

Canada
Summer-flowering tuberous begonias are probably better known, and more widely grown, than potted varieties, except the *semperflorens*. Soil, cool night temperatures, and coastal humid air produce some glorious flowering plants. The outdoor growing season is, of course, short. In Alberta, temperatures vary from 100° in summer to 40° below zero in winter.

Gorgeous specimens of rex begonias have been seen summering on porches on the Gaspé Peninsula. They often spend the winter on the same porches, glassed-in but not well heated, and—although dormancy is fairly general—they seem to thrive without the pampering of a central heating system.

Canadian winters are, admittedly, on the severe side: daylight hours are short; temperatures dip low. But lamps can be used to lengthen the days, and plants can be set back away from frosty windowpanes. Many a begonia grower would covet Canada's favorable summer temperature and humidity.

New England
The summer season is short, but cool nights on or near the coast produce glorious summer-blooming tuberous begonias. Other types can grow out-of-doors from about June 15 to September 1 in the northern, two weeks earlier and later in the southern, areas.

Soil is generally suitable for begonias, and good humus is often plentiful and easy to come by. Problems with unsuitable water are rare and isolated.

During the short days of northerly winter, keep temperature and humidity fairly high. Lengthen dark growing days with a few extra hours of light from reading or other lamps.

Middle Atlantic States

Here, the outdoor growing season is longer, but August can be hot enough to make growing the summer-blooming tuberous begonias tricky unless they are misted several times a day. Other begonias set outside for the summer will thrive in the light shade of a tall tree, or on the north or west side of house or tall hedge.

The only problem winter presents is the shortened day—and most potted plants react by simply resting until more hours of light come around naturally, in late winter or early spring. Generally—but not in all cases, or all areas—soil is on the acid side, acceptable to begonias.

Southeast

During hot and humid summer days, begonias need the shade of trees or lath house, and sometimes even cloth over the laths. Air can be cooled with hose spray, air-cooler system, or even—it's done all the time—by air-conditioning. Give plants plenty of space, good ventilation, extra drainage material in the bottom of pots. Don't sink pots in the soil; rather, set succulent types like *semperflorens* upon other, upturned pots or platforms.

Winter weather is nearly ideal for many types of begonias. Spanish moss or a covering of light cloth will provide protection against occasional freak frosts.

Sandy soil should be mixed with extra humus to make it light and fluffy. Growing in sphagnum moss has saved some rot-susceptible types for many growers. (See page 32.)

Midwest

Northerly, the summer outdoor season is short. Plants are set out after June 15, brought back inside by September 1. With extra cooling and humidifying effort, plants can survive where there are frequent or constant hot, dry winds; but it's not safe to leave them outside when you go on a long vacation. Sprinkle or spray plants and the surrounding area two or three times a day, to lower temperatures by evaporation.

Where winters are severe, keep plants several inches away from windowpanes, or "insulate" with sheets of newspaper or clear plastic.

Northwest

Cool nights produce giant summer tuberous-begonia blooms. Plants should be shaded from hot summer sun. Keep daytime air as cool and humid as possible. If soil is extremely sandy, add an extra ration of humus to help hold moisture.

In coldest winter, keep plants from touching glass in windows. Newspaper taped temporarily on panes will prevent frostbite of leaves and branch tips.

Southwest

The moist air and cool nights of California's and Texas's coastal areas constitute heaven for lovers of tuberous begonias. And most begonias of other types can be grown in gardens all year, with only slight and temporary setbacks in midwinter.

Since the welcome end of inland Texas's long drought, summer problems are less severe. Temperatures should be kept as low as possible around plants; humidity should be kept high by frequent misting or spraying, moist canvas or burlap curtains, or other devices. Sudden winter frosts perform freakish, but not usually fatal, pranks. Special soil preparations and fertilizers compounded especially for these areas are on the market.

CHAPTER 4

Propagating Begonias

If you've ever cut a "slip" from a wax begonia, put it in a glass of water, and watched roots form, fan out, and grow, you're no stranger to a plant's miraculous ability to reproduce itself. If you've thrown an apparently dead or dying plant on the compost heap or under a tree, and weeks later discovered that one small spark of life has sent up fresh new growth, you've witnessed evidence of a powerful "will to live." These are the qualities which keep renewing your interest in plants—every day a new shoot, a new root, a germinated seed, or signs of extraordinary rebirth.

Some delightful stories point up the wonders of plant propagation. Seeds of *Begonia cathcarti* have miraculously germinated after eighteen months in dark, forgotten storage. Quarter-inch sections of rotted rhizome or stem have been unknowingly left in the propagating medium, and look! A new shoot! Or how about the double- and multiruffled (but sterile) tuberous-begonia flowers which, near the end of summer, revert to single form and become fertile? And there's the unforgettable incident of the rex begonia seared by a greenhouse fire. The next day it spontaneously started to grow plantlets on its leaves—apparently, a desperate last attempt to perpetuate itself.

But enough of romance. There's the practical side to plant propagation—increasing your begonia collection with seeds and cuttings; exchanging with other growers; having new plants on hand for impromptu gifts or contributions to the plant table at church or club. If you're one of those who just can't bear to discard a living leaf or stem, you're always happily supplied with small plants for any worthy purpose.

THE PROPAGATING BOX

Why not look around, right now, for a place to put a "prop box"? You can use it so many ways—for germinating seeds, rooting cuttings of all kinds, nursing ailing plants, sheltering new arrivals until they recover from the shock of moving. It's simple to make, pleasant to look at, handy to have around, and costs incredibly little.

There's nothing new about the prop box like those pictured below. The design is not even mine. The principles which make it work are as old as the Wardian case. It protects tender seedlings and rooting cuttings from drafts, cold, and dry air.

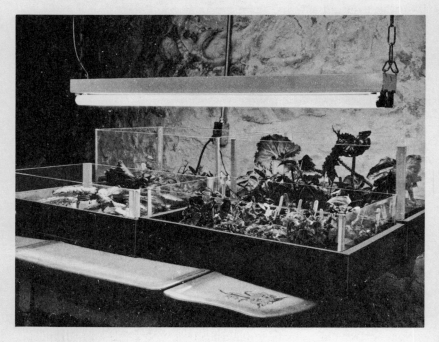

Propagating boxes inexpensively made from cherry crates and window glass, in cellar under fluorescent lights.

The frame is a cherry crate donated by the grocer. The sides are window glass, cut to measure at the hardware store, and held together at the corners with masking tape. Sharp edges are dulled by tape around the top, and around the glass used to cover the top. The box is lined, three inches deep, with a double thickness of the kitchen variety of aluminum foil. This can be fashioned into a one-piece tray to keep moisture from watermarking any surface the box is set on.

In the bottom of the box is a three-inch layer of moist propagating medium—vermiculite, leaf mold, peat, sand (or a substitute), either alone or mixed with one of the others. Half peat and half sand is a stand-by. Equal proportions of finely milled sphagnum, sand, and peat is a new recipe which makes the most of the best qualities of the three ingredients. For begonias, a propagating medium should be coarse and light enough to allow some air to reach the rooting stems, to ward off rot.

A more decorative affair can be arranged in an aquarium, with a piece of glass or kitchen plastic for the top. A more temporary, less tidy setup is a flat or shallow box with wire coat hangers fastened, upside down, at each end; these make a frame to support a drape of a thin sheet of Polyethylene. Or you can use the clear plastic in which your clothes are delivered from the dry cleaner's. A prop box can be plain or fancy, of any size or shape, finished fine or rough. Once you have one of any kind, you'll wonder how you ever kept plants without it.

Place your prop box anywhere except in the cold, the dark, or the bright sun. On top of the electric refrigerator, it will get no-cost bottom heat. Or there are low-cost heating coils which plug into ordinary electric outlets. Near the furnace in the cellar, with minimum daylight or artificial light, the box is warm but out of the way.

Small-scale variations of the prop box can be rigged up over a few cuttings inserted in rooting medium in a pot. Then, take your choice of humidifying tops: a plastic carrot bag; a tumbler; even waxed paper. Or a plastic bread box comes complete with transparent cover. In such smaller devices, if beads of moisture form inside the glass or plastic, loosen or lift it slightly so some air can circulate.

METHODS OF BEGONIA PROPAGATION

Begonias can be propagated in nearly every known way, and in some ways peculiarly their own. New plants can be grown by: sowing seed; rooting leaf, stem, rhizome cuttings; dividing old plants or tubers; even layering. Propagating procedures in this chapter are outlined for begonias in general. Chapters 6 through 15 cover when and how these principles vary for specific types of begonias.

Potting soil for young seedlings or newly rooted cuttings should be especially light, to encourage root growth, with even better drainage than ordinarily. It should not contain fertilizer, nor should young plants be fertilized until they are well on their way to maturity.

GROWING BEGONIAS FROM SEED

By this intriguing process you can collect many costly plants for next to nothing—or, by hybridizing, you can create new begonia varieties. Through its seed fund, the American Begonia Society has introduced hundreds of otherwise unavailable begonias. Many seed stores and catalogues also carry a representative selection. Some sources of begonia seeds are listed in the Appendix.

Begonia seeds are of two types. Seeds of begonia species—natural plants which have not been cross-pollinated by insects or human hands—will produce seedlings of nearly perfect uniformity. But from hybrids—varieties created by mating one begonia with another— you can expect some surprises; they will not "come true." Hybrid seeds are usually clearly marked, and often carry notations such as "50 per cent double," or "70 per cent variegated." This means that approximately half the plants will have double flowers, or about two thirds may have variegated leaves. Rex begonias have the most complicated ancestry of all. Seldom does a rex seed pod produce even two plants alike.

With favorable conditions, most begonia seeds will germinate in ten days to two weeks. But some of the more delicate varieties may take three months or more. Don't discard planted seed too soon; there is still hope for at least a year. And if you want quantities of plants from one planting, transplant seedlings carefully and replace the container, so that more seeds may germinate later. No matter how long the germination time, the planting medium must never become powder-dry.

Wax begonias are sown at any time of year; summer-blooming tuberous begonias, from December through March; most others grow more readily when planted at the beginning of the spring growing season. To be on the safe side, plant half the contents of a seed packet and reserve the rest for insurance.

Don't take chances with "damp-off" or "damping-off," a fungus disease which can mow down hundreds of healthy seedlings in a single swoop. Never plant begonia seeds in anything but clean containers and sterilized soil, or sterile planting mediums.

Step-by-Step Seed Sowing and Growing

The photograph on page 50 illustrates the complete process. Paragraph numbers here tie in with the numbers on the photograph.

1 In a clean container (plastic refrigerator dish, casserole, foil frozen-pie pan) place an inch or less of moist, finely sifted, sterilized soil. Topping with a thin layer of moist, finely milled sphagnum moss will make sure the surface is smooth enough for powder-fine seeds. Scatter seeds sparingly and evenly; do not cover with soil or sphagnum. Cover the container with glass or plastic, label it, and set it in a warm but not necessarily light place. Bottom heat appreciably speeds up germination. Don't allow seeds to chill below 65°; and don't allow them to dry out. Check daily; if the soil looks dry, water with a few drops on the side of the container.

2 When seeds start to germinate, uncover the container and set in a protective humidifying device—your prop box, a plastic box lined with moist paper toweling, or a temporary tent of kitchen plastic. Keep the seedlings warm and provide good light, but not strong sunlight. Continue to keep the soil moist.

3 When the seedlings have three leaves (the third is the first "true" begonia leaf) lift the tiny plants carefully on the pointed tip of nail file or paring knife, and place them in small, prepared holes in moist, fine, sterile soil. Firm it gently around the roots. The new container should have drainage holes so that bottom watering is possible. Holes can be punched in plastic with a hot ice pick or awl. To water, set the container in water to the rim until the top of the soil is just moist.

4 A space-saving "flat" is a plastic ice-cube tray which holds fourteen or more small plants. When seedlings grow so large that their leaves touch, transplant to small pots or an ordinary flat. Start weekly feedings with quarter-strength fertilizer solution.

5 Many unusual begonias are easily grown from seed, and many of these are hard to acquire in any other way, or for such a low cost. Seeds are also an inexpensive source of hundreds of single *semperflorens* varieties, called "bedding begonias," for edging flower beds, decorating porches and patios, filling window boxes, and dozens of other outdoor gardening purposes. *Semperflorens* begonias will bloom in six months from seed. Other types usually take longer.

Growing begonias from seed: 1. Planting in plastic refrigerator dish. 2. Germinated seeds in protective box, with moist paper towels. 3. First transplanting to small tray or plate. 4. Second transplanting from ice-cube tray to small pots. 5. Some begonias grown from seed—*vellozoana*, unnamed rex, bedding *semperflorens*.

STEM CUTTINGS

This is the usual method of propagating most upright and branching begonias, including *semperflorens,* angel-wing, hairy-leaved, some odd and rare, and most trailing varieties. General rules are outlined here. Specific suggestions for different plants and types of plants will be found in Chapters 6 through 15.

Stem cuttings seem to root more readily and make more vigorous plants if they are taken in early spring, when the parent plants are starting new growth. Tip cuttings include two nodes (the swollen joints on the stem from which leaves and branches grow). Longer cuttings of some types (such as angel-wing) can be divided into sections, each with at least four nodes, two to be inserted into the rooting medium and two to be left above. Remove flowers, buds, and all except smaller top leaves, so the cutting can save its strength for making roots.

Stem cuttings may or may not need the protection of the prop box. Some delicate varieties can't cope with dry air and drafts, and demand extra protection and humidity. Stronger growers, such as the *semperflorens* and angel-wings, will root in a glass of water—if, by the way, your water does not contain chemicals which slow up or prevent rooting. If juicy, succulent stems persist in rotting before they root, try dipping the cut in a mild Fermate solution.

When several roots have grown one inch long or more, pot the cutting in a light soil mix that contains no fertilizer. Keep it on the dry side until you see signs of new growth. For bushier plants in a hurry, place several rooted cuttings in one pot. As you pot a rooted cutting, gently firm the soil so as not to jerk the roots away from the stem.

LAYERING

Layering is the safe and sure way to propagate the begonias which droop branches on or near the soil. With a hairpin, or something similar, firmly pin down the third or fourth node (counting from the branch tip) onto the soil in the pot, or in another pot set beside the parent plant. When roots have formed, cut the stem between roots and parent; pot the new plant in the usual way.

Rhizomatous begonias may also be layered. The rhizome is pinned down so that at least one "eye"—or scar where root or stem grew out—touches the soil. When it has sent roots well down, the piece of rhizome is cut off cleanly and potted.

LEAF CUTTINGS

Although rhizome cuttings produce new plants more quickly and surely, rhizomatous begonias are more often propagated by leaf cuttings, to avoid chopping up a valuable specimen, or to produce a greater number of young plants from one stock plant. Winter-blooming tuberous begonias, and some of the oddities, are also propagated from leaf cuttings.

Here, let's clear up some confusion. Rex begonias are rhizomatous. They propagate freely from both rhizome and leaf cuttings. But their leaves form new plants in their own unique manner, described in Chapter 12. Leaf-cutting information given here is based on experience with non-rex rhizomatous begonias, winter tuberous, and some others. Special notes for these various types of begonias are included in their own special chapters.

Which begonia varieties are good subjects for leaf cuttings? The list would be long, and not particularly homogeneous. If you're in doubt, try. If you fail once, try at least once more. The fault may be something other than the plant variety. If you fail twice, chances are that your plant prefers to propagate in some other manner.

Unlike stem cuttings which—from the first new leaf—closely resemble the parent plant, leaf cuttings may take some time to reproduce the desired coloring, blotches, ruffles, or other plant personality traits. For example, as many as thirty round leaves have been known to appear on a plant grown from a "star" leaf before the typical star-shaped leaves appeared.

How To Take Leaf Cuttings

Cut firm, healthy leaves with one or two inches of stem attached. Some hardier varieties need nothing more than the stem end in a glass of water, the leaf resting on the rim. Others, which need prop box protection, are inserted with the stem half in and half out of the propagating medium, the leaf neither horizontal nor vertical, but slanted backward at an angle.

Roots start to form at the end of the stem in one to two weeks. Within six weeks or two months, new plants should appear on the stem. These can be carefully taken off and potted, and the mother leaf can be replaced, to make more plantlets—sometimes as many as three or four times. Protect the newly potted plantlets in a prop box until they are well established, with at least two sets of new leaves.

Occasionally, leaf cuttings will make roots, but no plants appear. Try taking another leaf with a "heel" at the end of the stem—a sliver from the branch it grew out of. A new plant may grow out of the leaf bud where leaf stem and plant stem meet.

A number of plants produced at the same time on the same leaf cutting, planted together in one pot, will make a thick, bushy new plant in the shortest time.

RHIZOME CUTTINGS

Because they propagate from rhizome cuttings in the same or similar manner, rex begonias are included with other rhizomatous begonias in this section.

Rhizome tip cuttings are taken from the pointed ends of the thick, scarred rhizomes. Each cutting should have at least one "eye" on top, and one on the bottom. After tip cuttings have been taken off, the parent plant quickly fills out with new growth.

Sectional rhizome cuttings are divisions of long pieces of rhizome, which leave the parent plant somewhat bereft. Cut the rhizome into two- or three-inch pieces, each with at least one eye over and one under. If the parent's rhizome is the kind that crawls along the top of the soil, some cuttings may come off complete with roots and can be potted immediately.

On both tip and sectional rhizome cuttings, remove larger leaves. Dust the open cuts with a disinfectant, such as sulfur. Insert rhizome pieces in prop box or other protective humidifying device. Cuttings from plants whose rhizomes grow horizontally are laid horizontal— half in and half out of the rooting medium. Upright growing rhizomes are inserted with the end not more than a half-inch deep in the medium, the rest of the cutting upright at a slanting angle.

Particularly during damp weather, fleshy rhizomes may have a tendency to rot. Disinfecting is an important precaution. Another is to have the rooting medium moist when cuttings are first inserted;

Begonia cuttings: 1. Stem cutting of 'Templini' kept warm and humid inside Polyethylene bag. 2. Plastic bread box holds rooting leaves of 'It.' 3. Rhizome tip cutting, 'Bunchi,' prepared for propagating. 4. Stem cutting of angel-wing *coccinea* ready for rooting in water. 5. Rooted leaf stands like an umbrella over new plantlet, 'Erythrophylla.' 6. Portion of 'Bunchi' leaf has made strong roots, small plant.

then allow it to dry out gradually, until the ends of the cuttings have scarred and healed over. The medium should be barely moist, never wet and soggy.

When roots have grown down from the rhizome into the medium below, pot the cuttings—at the same angle at which they were inserted for propagation—in a light soil mix containing no fertilizer. Water thoroughly; pamper the plantlet in a prop box, with the least possible watering, until it has made at least two new leaves of fair size.

DIVISION

Because most begonias propagate so readily in other ways, without mutilating the parent, division is an infrequent practice. Occasionally it is advisable—on older wax begonias, for example, which have grown a monstrous number of branches; or rhizomatous varieties which are pot-bound in the largest container you own.

Stems or rhizomes, and roots, are gently separated at the soil level. Each division is potted in a suitable size of new container.

Division of begonia tubers is discussed in Chapter 15.

CHAPTER 5

Begonia Problems and Pests

"What's wrong with my plants?" This question comes from all kinds of growers, amateurs and professionals. Plant pathologists, like doctors, have to see the patient in order to prescribe. Describing the symptoms may help a little, or it may not. Suppose your plant has spots on the leaves. These could be caused by a fungus disease, scorching sun, or improper watering. Gray dust? It may mildew—or just dust. The plant is slowly pining away? It may be hungry or overfed, sick or dormant.

If you have any authority to turn to—someone on the staff of your horticultural society, a professional gardener, the extension service at your state university, your county agricultural agent—by all means arrange for a consultation. Take or send your plant along, or at least a leaf, flower, or stem showing the troublesome spots. Be ready with a report of cultural conditions—temperature, light, soil, and the like. Even the most experienced expert needs complete information.

And don't think you're the only grower who's ever hovered over an ailing plant. Insects and diseases are part of Nature's system, and few plants are immune. Nor are begonias the only plants which are subject to problems and pests. Actually, because they're happy in most home growing conditions, begonias suffer much less than many other kinds of plants.

If expert advice is not available, and you must be your own plant doctor, make sure your methods are as nearly expert as the information in this chapter—and from other sources—can make them.

And don't be discouraged if you are not always able to save a precious plant. Even the experts are stumped, for example, by "dieback"—a mysterious condition which causes a plant thriving in perfect cultural conditions to collapse and die overnight. Someday, science will find the fatal bug or fungus which causes so much anguish.

PREVENTION

Whether your plants inhabit a window sill, sun porch, greenhouse, or conservatory, infections can be cut down—if not cut out—by sound preventive measures.

Hygiene

Clean tools, pots, flats don't carry disease. Rotting leaves, flowers, stems do. Many epidemics spread as your hands touch one plant and then another. Fanatical cleanliness saves work and worry in the long run.

Isolation

Any suspected plant should be whisked away from its companions until your suspicions are confirmed or not. New arrivals should be set apart from other plants for at least two weeks—the time it takes most insects to grow large enough to be seen.

Ventilation

Fresh air is a fumigant of sorts. Stale, stagnant air breeds trouble, particularly when humidity is high. Disease spreads fast when plants are crowded so close together that air can't circulate freely.

Vigilance

Keep one eye always on tender buds or new tip growth, where so many ills first get a foothold. Examine with a magnifying glass. Spot the critters while they're young and vulnerable; the disease before it can spread. Never let up on strict preventive measures.

HOW TO EXAMINE A PLANT

Start at the top, the new tip growth. Is it fresh-colored, firm, and crisp—or is it disfigured, or soft and spongy? With the magnifying glass or without, can you see any signs of insect life?

Next, step back a little. Look at the leaves and flowers. Are colors fresh, healthy, and true? Is an edge crinkled where it should be smooth? Are there any unsightly spots? Have buds dropped before opening? Check the stems for blemishes too.

Now, unless you've arrived at a quick conclusion, turn the plant out of the pot and examine the roots. If the ends are dry, dark, dead-looking, the roots are not able to feed the plant above. Healthy rootlets are tender, crisp, light-colored. If the plant grows from a tuber or rhizome, it should feel firm and springy.

Soggy, sour-smelling, mushy soil is another factor. And so are the insects or worms you might find as you dig into it.

When you've given an ailing plant a thorough going-over, you're prepared to consult this or any other reference, to diagnose the trouble and find out what you can do to remedy it.

COMBATING PROBLEMS AND PESTS

Treatment can be simple or complicated, mild or stringent, depending on your preference and the severity of your problem. For some insects and diseases, a heavy water spray—or holding the plant upside down and swishing it around in warm water—is effective if repeated regularly until all symptoms have disappeared. Soapy water has some insecticidal properties and will wash away some sources of infection plus foot-loose insects and some fungus growths.

Dusting, dipping, or spraying with a disinfectant, fungicide, or insecticide works faster and more thoroughly—on more types of pestilence—and is certainly called for when an infection is deep-seated or widespread.

Here, some vital words of caution. No matter how safe a preparation may be, or how highly recommended, try it first on a few plants. Make sure you are using the proper methods, in proper conditions, to avoid damaging plants.

Read every word of the label, down to the fine-print list of ingredients. Is this preparation recommended for house plants? Or is it marked "Garden Spray," or "Household Insect Spray"? Outdoor garden plants can take tougher treatment—and so can indoor insects like flies and mosquitoes. And find out whether this treatment is specifically recommended to fight the kind of insect or disease your plant is afflicted with. A spray for mildew won't bother mites sucking your plant's life away; nor will a miticide work much of a cure on mildew.

Equally vital—if not more so—follow package directions to the last dotted "i" and crossed "t." Stick to the recommended proportions, carriers, containers, methods of application, and aftercare. Protect children and pets against any possible poisoning.

Dusting

Whether to dust or spray is a matter of choice, and of available material. Some treatments are made only in powdered form; and some people simply prefer to dust. On the other hand, some dusts, remaining on plants, will discolor flowers and leaves. Find out about this factor first.

Modern plastic squeezer-duster containers are handy for treating small groups of plants. Dusters (get the best you can afford; it's a wise investment in the long run) are more economical for larger numbers of plants, as in a greenhouse. With some practice, you can develop a facility in laying on the dust thinly, evenly, on both sides of leaves and around stems and flowers. Dusts are usually left on plants because they have some lasting effect.

Spraying

Good sprayers (buy the best, if you can) come in a number of different types and sizes. Select one that's suitable for your growing conditions and the number of plants you grow. When you fill a sprayer, be sure to follow the directions on the package of spray material. Adding a small amount of a mild household detergent may be recommended to speed up spreading.

Usually, sprays are most effective at a temperature between 60° and 80°—and most safe when applied out-of-doors, if at all possible. Spray steadily over, under, and around leaves, flowers, and stems. Make sure the spray penetrates dense growth. Wet the top of the soil or drench it thoroughly, if the insect or disease is likely to find refuge in the soil.

After spraying, let the plant stand and drain for an hour or two; then rinse it gently—unless package directions advise otherwise.

To clear up an infection completely, re-apply insecticides and fungicides at the number of regular intervals recommended on the package.

Aerosol bombs are easy and neat to use—if costly for large numbers of plants—but can do more harm than good if package directions are ignored. It is important to keep the bomb eighteen inches away from the plant. Sweep the can up and around, and under leaves, to cover all parts of the plant.

Shaving cream, dentifrice, or bug-killer—Aerosol cans look so much alike, take care not to pick up a household insect bomb, instead of the house-plant spray you meant to use or buy.

Dipping

Immersing a plant, upside down, in a pan, pail, or sinkful of spray solution will often cover all plant parts and surfaces more completely than a handy spray. It's also easier when a number of plants are to be treated, or when a plant has extremely branching and dense growth.

With small pots, hold in the soil with spread fingers, then upend the plant and slosh it gently around in the spray solution. Set it aside to drain; then immerse it in a lukewarm-water rinse. To help keep soil in larger pots, hold a piece of plastic or foil over the surface as you dip the plant.

Plants can also be dipped upright. Simply set pot and all in solution deep enough to cover it. Since this method also saturates the soil, it is recommended for treating diseases which originate in the soil, or insects which are harbored there.

Insecticides

Some of the chemical insecticides listed here are sold and used on their own; many are mixed with others in multipurpose sprays for house plants; some are sold under other, registered brand names. All are poisonous to insects, and sometimes in some degree to man. Check the label to make sure the ingredients are specifically recommended for use against your specific infestation.

Reliable insecticides usually combined with one or more others are: butoxide, lindane, methoxychlor, pyrethrum, rotenone. Chlordane and DDT may be used separately or in combination. Nicotine sulfate is a standard contact poison for sucking insects. Sodium selenate is a systemic insecticide. When applied to the soil, it is taken up into the plant, which becomes poisonous to insects which eat it. VC_{13} is a systemic nematocide—a specific for nematodes. Metaldehyde is the poison in snail and slug baits.

Miticides—insecticides specifically to combat mites—are available under brand names such as Aramite, Dimite, Kelthane. Check the label for anti-mite ingredients like malathion or parathion.

Fungicides

Many plant diseases are caused by growth and spread of fungus organisms. Sulfur is often used as a disinfectant. New fungicides which deposit a preventive residue but don't disfigure foliage and flowers include: Fermate, Captan, Karathane.

BEGONIA CLINIC

For quick reference, the common symptoms of the most common begonia ailments—caused by poor cultural conditions, or fungus or insect infestation—are keyed to the numbered sections describing the problems, which follow.

For these symptoms:	*Check sections:*
Buds deformed	29, 35
drop before opening	3, 8, 9, 11
Flowers few or none	1, 2, 4, 5, 15, 17, 18, 32
deformed	29, 35
Leaves rot	7, 23
have mold	7, 20
discolored on top	6, 21, 27, 30, 31
discolored on undersides	22, 35
drop	3, 8, 10, 12, 19, 21, 27, 29, 30
deformed	24, 29
chewed ragged	34
poor color	2, 4, 17
poor texture	1, 2, 11, 17, 20
raised blisters	10
edges dry, brown	8, 16, 17
few and small	15, 17
Plant suddenly collapses	2, 3, 14, 19, 23
dies gradually	12, 19, 23, 32, 33
does not grow	2, 6, 12, 15, 17, 18, 19, 25, 28, 29, 32
grows lopsided, lanky	4
wilts	1, 10, 11, 13, 25
Roots brown, broken	16
rotted	10, 14, 23
knots on	32
Soil dries too slowly	2, 7, 10
dries too fast	1, 13

For these symptoms:	Check sections:
Stems long, limp, flabby	4, 14
wilt	11
have mold	7, 20
white-dotted	28
rot	7, 23
Tip growth wilts, withers	10
dry, brown	12, 16
deformed	24

Cultural Problems

Sometimes (and some varieties of) begonias will react sharply to unfavorable conditions; in other situations (and with other begonias) there may be only an over-all malaise or unhealthy appearance. The most prevalent reactions are covered here. If general unhealthiness is the only symptom, check Chapter 3, on culture, or the chapter devoted to the group to which the problem plant belongs.

1 TEMPERATURE TOO HIGH. *Symptoms:* Leaves feel and look dry, lifeless; not supple and alive. Plant wilts frequently; needs watering more than once a day. Few or no flowers at usual flowering time of year.

2 TEMPERATURE TOO LOW. *Symptoms:* Plant "stands still"—lives, but does not grow or bloom. Leaves have a sickly color, feel limp.

Delicate *bartonea* loves warmth, humidity—can suddenly shrivel and die back in chill drafts.

Soil takes too long to dry out. Plant may appear to be in good health one day, flop over and die the next.

3 TEMPERATURE TOO CHANGEABLE. *Symptoms:* Unopened buds and leaves drop. Plant may suddenly collapse. *Cause:* Chill drafts in warm air, or extreme jumps from cold to warm—plant suffers "shock." Occasionally results when plant is moved from warm, humid greenhouse to cool, dry home.

4 LIGHT TOO WEAK. *Symptoms:* Stems limp, soft, and longer than normal with exaggerated spaces between nodes. Leaves lack fresh, healthy color; look pale, wan; unhealthy sheen. Plant stretches toward the light, blooms little or not at all. *Treatment:* Cut back and start over; provide more light. *Note:* All window-sill-grown plants, even with strong light, will tend to lean in the direction of the one light source. To preserve symmetry, rotate pots a quarter-turn every day or so.

With insufficient light, plants stretch out, grow straggly. 'Preussen' should also have been pinched out to promote bushy growth.

5 INSUFFICIENT SUNLIGHT. *Symptom:* Plant bloomed well last winter, but hasn't a flower this year. *Cause:* Check last winter's weather reports. Were there fewer sunless days with dark, over-cast skies? This year, how many days of really bright sunlight?

SEMPERFLORENS BEGONIAS

TOP ROW: 'Pistachio,' 'Curly Locks,' 'Flamingo.' MIDDLE ROW: Single-flowering red, 'Green Thimble,' 'Cinderella,' 'Red Camellia.' BOTTOM ROW: Calla-lily 'Pink Jewel,' 'Ballet,' Calla-lily 'Ruby Jewel.'

Treatment: Try a few bonus hours of artificial light beginning at twilight every day.

6 SUNLIGHT TOO STRONG. *Symptoms:* Thin, brown spots on leaves —sunscald. Plant looks shriveled, stunted; leaves are reddish, even scorched. *Treatment:* To prevent sunscald, avoid water on leaves when plant is in sun. Otherwise, move plants out of strong sunlight, or provide some shade.

7 AIR STALE, TOO HUMID. *Symptoms:* Filmy mold forms around base of stems, particularly on cuttings rooting in closed prop box. Leaves rot, starting at center and working out to edge. Stems become squashy and rot off. Soil is sour, seldom dries out. *Treatment:* Increase circulation of fresh air. Space plants well apart. Partially remove top from prop box; keep propagating medium on dry side.

8 AIR TOO DRY, HUMIDITY TOO LOW. *Symptoms:* Leaves continually drop; new leaves form. Leaf edges are crisp, dried. Flower buds don't develop, or fall before opening. *Treatment:* Provide more humidity. (See page 26.)

9 LEAKING GAS. Many ills blamed on gas are really caused by some other cultural problem. If buds don't open into flowers, and you suspect gas leakage, set a tomato plant in the same area. If there is escaping gas, the tomato plant will droop, leaves curl down and discolor. Unless the leak is severe, careful ventilation will suffice. Of all types, propane or "bottled" gas is the least noxious to plants.

10 TOO MUCH WATER, TOO OFTEN. *Symptoms:* Soil is constantly muddy; roots and rhizomes rot. Healthy plants (especially hairy-leaved varieties) suddenly wilt, wither, dry at top. Lower leaves (particularly angel-wings) drop off as if cut from stem, leaving small tassel of new leaves at tip. Leaves have blistery, dropsy-type swellings (oedema). *Treatment:* Make sure pot has adequate drainage. Hold back water, even to the point of wilting. Never water on dark, damp days. When plant looks ill, start new cuttings in a hurry. One small but firm and living section of rhizome or root can often be trimmed clean and started again in prop box.

11 TOO LITTLE WATER, TOO SELDOM. *Symptoms:* Leaves and stems wilt. Well-formed flower buds drop off. Leaves (particularly summer-blooming tuberous begonias) wither and dry, without

Kept too moist, angel-wing 'Pink Parade' drops its lower leaves.

turning yellow first. *Cause:* Is soil too sandy? Is pot so full that water has no room to wait until it can seep down and soak the root ball? Are you watering thoroughly, so that excess runs out the bottom—or merely wetting the top inch or so? Do you water on a set schedule, or when plants actually need it? *Treatment:* Most begonias wilted from dryness will perk up amazingly fast when soil and pot are soaked in pan or bowl of water up to the rim.

12 SOIL TOO HEAVY. *Symptoms:* Plant "doesn't do well," barely survives. New tip growth withers, dries. Plant gradually dies. In hot, dry weather (and especially in summer-flowering tuberous begonias) the lower leaves yellow and fall off. *Treatment:* Turn soil out of pot, examine roots. Clean off any that look dark and dead. Repot in fresh soil. Prune back severely. If this is one of the more delicate begonias, try it in a wire hanging basket lined with moss, and a lighter soil mix containing more humus. Or try sphagnum moss (see page 32).

13 SOIL TOO LIGHT. *Symptoms:* Plant requires too-frequent water-ing, has tendency to wilt several times a day, particularly in hot weather. *Treatment:* Mix soil that will hold more moisture,

Rex 'Helen Lewis' wilts when dried out . . .

. . . revives quickly when pot is soaked in water to its rim.

increasing proportion of humus and cutting down on or omitting sand. If possible, use soil containing more clay.

14 POT TOO LARGE. *Symptoms:* Stems grow flabby and wither. Plant may collapse. Roots rot and decay. Soil turns sour. *Cause:* Too much soil supplies more food than roots can absorb, retains too much water, admits insufficient air.

15 POT TOO SMALL. *Symptoms:* No new growth, especially in summer. Few or no flowers. Leaves sparse and small. *Cause:* Plant is starved for food and new soil.

16 TOO MUCH FERTILIZER. *Symptoms:* Accumulated white fertilizer salts on soil surface form a crust so hard it can cut tender stems. Leaf edges brown and crisp (particularly in summer-flowering tuberous begonias). Tip growth crisp, brown—first sign of "fertilizer burn." When turned out of pot, roots look brown and dry, break off with small bits of soil. *Treatment:* Severe damage requires repotting in fresh soil, even flushing old soil from roots with hard water stream; and, of course, withholding fertilizer. For less serious cases, scrape off top layer of soil, flush water through from top to bottom, top-dress with fresh soil.

17 INSUFFICIENT FERTILIZER. *Symptoms:* No growth, no flowers, especially in summer. Leaves few and small. Leaves may pucker and crack on edge, indicating lack of potash, phosphorous, or both—supply superphosphate. Leaves colored yellow-green to yellow usually show nitrogen deficiency. Check the ingredients on the label of your fertilizer container.

18 POOR STOCK. *Symptoms:* Rooted, potted cutting does not grow. Despite good cultural conditions, mature plant refuses to grow or flower. *Cause:* Some cuttings get a poor start in life, lack sufficient root system to feed plant properly. Try a new cutting; or reset the youngling with stem deeper in soil, so new roots can form along the side. Also, there are occasionally plants from apparently healthy stock which turn out to be "poor growers" or "poor bloomers." Try everything cultural once. If the plant does not respond, discard in favor of a new start.

19 DORMANCY. *Symptoms:* Plant either looks droopy, tired, does not grow; or (particularly with rex and other rhizomatous varieties) drops its leaves in quick succession. *Cause:* Many plants "rest" at some time every year—begonias usually in fall and early winter. *Treatment:* Water sparingly; withhold fertilizer completely; do not repot; set plant where it will be protected, out of strong light. In spring, watch for new leaves and other signs of new growth. Then, repot with fresh soil, resume regular watering and fertilizing. *Note:* You can usually tell whether a rhizomatous begonia is dying or going dormant by gently pinching the rhizome with your fingers. If it feels firm and alive—not soft and rotten—the diagnosis is probably dormancy.

Diseases. Fuss-budget insistence on cleanliness is both prevention and cure for diseases caused by fungi or bacteria. Available disinfectants and fungicides help control infections and their spread; but your best bet is to keep plants clean and healthy.

20 BOTRYTIS. *Symptoms:* Gray mold on leaves and stems, usually in moist greenhouse. Leaves feel watery. *Cause:* Rapid-spreading fungus thrives in stale air, high humidity, insufficient light; feeds on dead plant parts on soil, shelf, bench. *Treatment:* Keep fresh air circulating. Remove and destroy dead leaves, stems, flowers. Avoid misting leaves. Cut off infected parts cleanly; treat with Fermate or other fungicide.

21 BACTERIAL LEAF SPOT. *Symptoms:* (1) Small yellow circles on leaf surface which (2) turn brown with translucent margins, then (3) become black—and leaves drop. Stems may infect at nodes. *Cause:* Combined high temperature and humidity, usually in summer. *Treatment:* Prevent spread by isolating plant; do not root cuttings. Destroy organic debris. If possible, lower temperature and humidity; step up circulation of fresh air.

22 POWDERY MILDEW. *Symptoms:* Small, pale spots under leaves become chalky-looking; leaf is thin and brown in spots when "powder" is wiped off. In severe cases, light powder is ringed with red margin. Most apparent on lower, older leaves. Most likely to attack rexes, silver-leaved varieties in other groups, and summer-blooming tuberous begonias. *Cause:* Fungus runs rampant when temperatures are low and humidity high. *Treatment:* Water or spray early in the day, not late; isolate suspects; wash hands thoroughly before touching other plants. Apply sulfur dust or fungicide. Repeat at recommended intervals until disease disappears, temperature rises, humidity lowers.

23 ROT—STEM AND ROOT. *Symptoms:* Plant may wilt gradually or suddenly topple over as if cut off. Stems and tubers (in summer-flowering tuberous begonias) become slimy, soft. Rhizomes (in rhizomatous, rexes) rot. *Cause:* Brown mold in debris on soil contacts leaves or stem, spreads inside stems and even down into tubers. *Treatment:* Be fanatical about cleanliness. Sterilize soil. Ventilate, for good circulation of fresh air. Watch watering in damp, stuffy weather. Space plants well apart. No cure for badly infected plants; in others, cut out infected areas cleanly and dis-

infect with sulfur or fungicide. Spray or dust entire growing area with fungicide.

Insects. The few chewing and sucking insects with a predilection for tender, juicy begonia leaves and stems are not by any means the most destructive of the parasites in the plant world, nor the most difficult to get rid of. With today's scientific chemicals—and the new ones science will develop tomorrow, before this book is in your hands—prevention, control, and cure are almost a snap.

24 APHIDS. *Symptoms:* New tips and leaves curl; insects can be seen congregating on juicy new growth. *Cause:* Small, soft-bodied insects—green, red, brown, or black—suck sap from new growth. *Treatment:* Can be flushed or washed off, or routed with insecticide. Repeat at weekly intervals until all eggs are hatched. Or put crushed moth balls (or one tablespoon naphthalene flakes) in paper bag, close plant inside tightly for twenty-four hours. Repeat at intervals to take care of eggs.

25 EARTHWORMS. *Symptoms:* Plant is tired, listless, weak; wilts. *Cause:* In small pots, worms may break off new roots, cut down on food absorption; can also convert fibrous-textured soil to soggy and damp soil. *Treatment:* Discourage entry with crushed moth-ball or naphthalene flakes in drainage material in bottom of pot. Unless your soil mix is neutral or alkaline, water plants with a half-teaspoon lime in one quart water.

26 FLIES, BLACK. *Symptom:* Flies swarm when plant is disturbed. *Cause:* "Fungus gnats" live in decaying organic matter, sour soil. They're unpleasant, but do not damage plant. *Treatment:* Broken charcoal in drainage material or in soil mix keeps soil sweet. Do not overwater. Spray plant and saturate soil with insecticide.

27 FLIES, WHITE. *Symptoms:* Flies cluster under leaves, swarm when disturbed. May deposit sticky "honeydew." Leaves turn yellow and drop. *Cause:* Insects suck juices from under leaves. *Treatment:* Insecticidal spray, or dip, at one-week intervals.

28 MEALYBUGS. *Symptoms:* Waxy white, cottony dabs on stem where branches join. Plant is tired, limp. *Cause:* Mature females suck plant juices, weaken plant. *Treatment:* Remove with fingernail or swab dipped in alcohol. Or dip plant in nicotine insecticide, or malathion. Repeat four times at ten-day intervals to catch hatching eggs.

29 MITES, CYCLAMEN. *Symptoms:* Plants don't grow or flower properly. New leaves and buds are crinkled, deformed; flower petals may be streaked. Leaves feel brittle, fall off when touched. *Cause:* Nearly invisible, infectious insect feeds on tender growth of opening buds and leaves. *Treatment:* Miticide, following directions carefully. Sodium selenate in soil.

30 MITES, RED-SPIDER. *Symptoms:* Leaves turn yellow or brownish on top; underneath, yellowish-brown, with small white "spiderwebs" where veins join. Leaves become silvery-brown and drop off. Pest difficult to spot until injury is severe. *Cause:* Tiny insects assemble under leaves, suck sap, increase rapidly in hot, dry weather. *Treatment:* Apply miticide three times at one-week intervals, making sure to soak undersurface of leaves. Or, to be safe, destroy plant and pot.

31 NEMATODE, LEAF. *Symptoms:* Rusty-brown blotches on leaves enlarge until leaf dies. *Cause:* Microscopic worm feeds on leaf tissues. Overhead watering brings worms to surface, encourages spread. *Treatment:* Sodium selenate in soil. Prevent spread with hygiene. Space plants so leaves don't touch. Water only from below.

32 NEMATODE, ROOT-KNOT. *Symptoms:* Plant does not grow or flower; slowly dies. Stem at soil surface may show "warts." Large roots in soil disfigured by thickened knots. *Cause:* Tiny worms "blind" the plant beyond the point of attack; it can't take food or water through roots. Extremely infectious, and weakens plant's resistance to other pests and diseases. *Treatment:* Sterilize soil. Try nematicide. Ward off secondary infections with all-purpose sprays.

33 SCALE. *Symptoms:* Plant slowly grows weaker. Under leaves and near joints are clusters of red or brown flattened bodies which can be loosened with a pinpoint or knife blade. *Cause:* Many different scale insects suck vital plant juices. *Treatment:* Destroy badly infected leaves and stems. Wipe off leaf, scrape off scales, repeat every ten days. Or dip (not spray) in malathion or nicotine sulfate three to five times at weekly intervals.

34 SLUGS AND SNAILS. *Symptoms:* Leaf edges chewed ragged; young leaves may disappear completely. *Cause:* Snails and slugs (shell-less snails) of several types feed on tender growth at night. Eggs

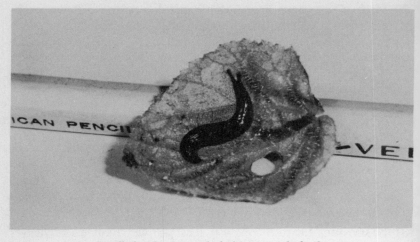

Small slug has eaten hole in *imperialis* leaf.

may hatch in soil. *Treatment:* Bait containing metaldehyde comes in drench, meal, or pellet form. Slug eats it, dies—and you dispose of the slimy corpse.

35 THRIPS. *Symptoms:* Rusty-brown or silvery-brown blotches under leaves where eggs are laid. Flowers (particularly summer-blooming tuberous begonias) are disfigured and discolored; buds open improperly. *Cause:* Small blue-gray or black insects suck life from plant. *Treatment:* All-purpose insecticide, malathion, sodium selenate.

CHAPTER 6

Semperflorens Begonias

Fondly nicknamed "wax" begonias, for their high-gloss leaves, or "semps" (abbreviation of the Latin *semperflorens,* "everblooming"), for their bustling year-round blooms, these are the begonias everybody knows and grows, or remembers from 'way back. They are among the easiest begonias to bring into flower, the most rewardingly colorful in bloom, and the most readily available from either local greenhouses or mail-order suppliers.

The semps are identified by some charming characteristics. They branch out freely, forming full and bushy plants which generally keep their size within sensible window-sill bounds. The stems are juicy and succulent-looking. The countless crisp, waxy leaves are more uniformly round than in other types of begonias; the veins radiate out from the stem end, rather than branching off at intervals. The typical begonia male and female flowers are bright and abundant, often seem to cover the little bush.

The succulence and shape of leaves and stems are an inheritance from the ancestral *Begonia semperflorens,* a species which was crossed, in 1878, with *B. schmidtiana* and has been relegated to obscurity, although the second parent is still grown today. From crossing the offspring with each other—and with other begonia species—the familiar old-time single-flowered wax begonia was developed. Most nineteenth-century homes harbored one or more of these blooming beauties. And they are still popular today, particularly for outdoor use in summer.

The next development introduced semps—still with single flowers —with dark bronzy-green or bronzy-red leaves. And today's sensational new semps have semidouble and double flowers in all shades from white to fiery red; with leaves green, bronze, or mahogany; from dwarf size to a foot tall. Popularly called "thimble," "rose," "rosebud," "camellia-flowered" begonias, these fancy charmers are probably the most grown and most desired house plants in America today.

Some fifty years ago, Nature played one of her most popular tricks, and produced mutations, or "sports," with green leaves streaked and splotched glistening white. The formation of pure white new leaves, as they unfold, gave this group the popular name "calla-lily begonias." These are striking plants which seldom fail to cause comments and compliments to the grower.

The semps are the friendliest plants in the world. They have a fresh, shining-clean look and plump, pleasant shape. They're eager to bloom almost all year, in a riot of gay colors, providing cheerful window-sill decoration with a minimum of care.

HOW TO GROW *Semperflorens* BEGONIAS

In a nutshell, here's how *semperflorens* culture compares with the general principles in Chapter 3: lower temperature, more light and sun, less moisture and humidity, heavier potting soil, smaller pots, more fertilizer. These differences are not major deviations, but slight degrees.

To sum up culture another way: *semperflorens* begonias grow and bloom best when the temperature is 70° or under; sunlight is full, except in the heat of midsummer; soil is allowed to dry out thoroughly before watering; the roots become pot-bound in soil containing more loam than humus; and feeding is on a regular schedule—a half-strength solution every two weeks, or full-strength monthly, except immediately after the flowering cycle has finished.

Of these conditions, sunshine is one of the most important. Without it, in fall and winter, there will be few—if any—flowers. Only in the hottest summer sun do the leaves discolor and crisp on the edges if they are in full sun.

Also important is the relative dryness of the soil and the air around semps. They are so like succulents, they will rot in a hurry if kept too moist. Let the soil dry out completely before watering; and never water on dark, damp, or rainy days.

Pinching and Pruning

Semperflorens begonias will grow more compact and bushy—and, because there will be more branches, will produce more abundant

Single *semperflorens* begonia

Crested, or Thimble   Double, or Rosebud

TYPICAL *SEMPERFLORENS* BEGONIAS

bloom—if they are pinched back at least once in their young life. This should be when eagerly growing seedlings or rooted cuttings are three to five inches tall, before flower buds appear.

The double-flowering varieties, and many of the singles, should be severely chopped back when peak flowering has passed. Don't think this is a heartless operation—it's a lifesaver that gives the plant a chance at new beauty. Try it. When flowering slackens and the plant begins to look a bit tired and straggly, lift up the lower leaves and look for the new shoots which will usually be coming up from the roots. Get your sharp knife, grit your teeth, and cut out all the old stems at the base—and see how soon the new growth produces a fresh, new, well-shaped plant and another cycle of bountiful flowers. The cuttings, of course, can be rooted to make more plants.

HOW TO PROPAGATE *Semperflorens* BEGONIAS

Except for leaf cuttings and layering, all the propagating methods described in Chapter 4 work easily and well for semps. Mature plants are particularly good subjects for division. Where the stems are slightly swollen, just under the top of the soil, cut the crown into several pieces, each with either one well-branched stem, or several smaller stems. Gently disentangle the roots, and put the new plants in small pots.

Seeds

Of all types of begonias, the single-flowering semps are the easiest to grow from seed—inspiring and rewarding for the beginner to begin with. Indeed, many will seed themselves in pots or in garden beds. The semidoubles and doubles are less reliable, and are not guaranteed to produce 100 per cent double or semidouble seedlings. Once they are an inch or so tall, seedling semps need less pampering than more touchy types, and very quickly take their place in pots on the window sill or in summer gardens.

Stem Cuttings

Most varieties of semps will root readily when the stems are simply slipped in a glass of water. The protection of a prop box is not only unnecessary, but may sometimes cause the cuttings to rot unless the propagating medium is nearly dry. In greenhouses, of course, these cuttings are rooted in sand or some special propagating mixture.

Cuttings may be taken at almost any time of year, and particularly when the plants are cut back after flowering. Basal cuttings usually make stronger plants than the new, soft tip growth—and are certainly less tricky to root.

There is one "trade secret" about selecting portions of double-flowering semps (and many singles too, for that matter) to be cut and rooted. Unless the cutting has at least one branch—unless it inherits the branching habit—it may likely grow tall and unbranched, no matter how much you pinch out. So take cuttings which branch at least once, if possible; and cut them as close to the soil level as you safely can.

Propagating *semperflorenes* begonias: 1. Crested-type 'Pistachio,' old stems cut back to soil after flowering, allowing new growth to come up from the base. 2. Cutting with branching habit is making bushy, well-branched plant. 3. Right way—stem cutting with branch. 4. Wrong way —cutting without branch may make spindly, single-stem plant.

NAMED VARIETIES OF *Semperflorens* BEGONIAS

This group of begonias is more homogeneous than any of the others. Whether the leaves are green or dark red, the flowers single or double, the size dwarf or tall, a semp is unmistakably a semp in anyone's eyes—which means that the number of distinct variations is necessarily limited, and that many nearly identical semps are sold under entirely different names, in different areas.

Because of the homogeneity of the *semperflorens* group—all have branching, bushy growth; waxy leaves; succulent stems—detailed varietal descriptions are not given in this chapter. And because all semps are relatively easy to grow, the described varieties are not grouped (as in other chapters) as beginners', advanced, and collectors' items. Instead, named varieties are grouped as single-flowering semps and double-flowering, and the calla-lily begonias have a separate section of their own. Varietal descriptions are short and (we hope) sweet.

SINGLE-FLOWERING SEMPS

Except for summer garden growing, these delightfully colorful plants have regrettably taken a back seat to the newer, more glamorous double-flowering varieties. But outdoors, in semisunny beds, they bloom their heads off from planting-out time to frost. They make neat, bushy borders; some of the taller, larger-leaved varieties are used as accent or for foundation plantings. They cost practically nothing when grown (and so easily) from seed; require a priceless minimum of care. Removing dried flowers and seed pods is a small attention they appreciate but by no means demand.

Try edging a flower bed with a neat row of similar-sized semps of the same flower and foliage color, or alternate plants of contrasting colors. Or mix all available harmonious tints. In late summer, take cuttings to be potted for window-sill bloom in winter. They'll root right in the soil under a tree or shrub.

These are some of the named varieties of single-flowering *semperflorens* begonias available—plants or seeds—from suppliers in various parts of the country.

'Adeline'—Sometimes listed as 'Improved Darling.' Dwarf with single pink flowers, green leaves.
'Andy'—Dwarf, for bedding; flowers, luminous pink; leaves grass-green.
'Blütenmeer'—Bronze leaves; flowers rose-pink, medium size. One

of the group of 'gracilis' semps developed in Germany, extremely compact with small foliage.

'Bois de Vaux'—'Gracilis' type with rose flowers, green leaves.

'Bonfire'—Furious bloomer with dark red leaves, scarlet flowers.

'Carmen'—Dark bronze leaves; pink flowers.

'Christmas Cheer'—Rose-red flowers; green leaves.

'Fiesta'—A novelty with large-petaled red flowers centered with a gorgeous golden powder puff of pollen.

'Flamingo'—Novelty, extra-large white flowers, edged with red; green leaves.

'Indian Maid'—Red foliage; cerise-orange flowers.

'Karin' (also called 'Frosty' or 'Indian Bride')—Bronze leaves; white flowers.

'Organdy'—Large flowers of different shades of pink, rose, salmon, red, white on one plant.

'Pink Profusion'—Green leaves; pink flowers.

'Red Pearl'—Glowing red flowers; green leaves.

'Red Perfection'—Fiery flowers; green leaves.

'Sparkler'—Foliage bronzy-red; flowers orange-salmon.

'Tausendschoen' ('Thousand Beauties')—Actually, a group of dwarf-growing semps outlandishly bushy for their size, covered with countless flowers in your choice of red, pink, or white.

'White Pearl'—Green leaves; chaste white flowers.

'Winter Romance'—Foliage light green; flowers pink and white; dwarf habit.

SEMIDOUBLE-FLOWERING SEMPS

These are actually single flowers which decided to become double but stopped along the way, when they developed delightful "crested" or "thimble" flowers. The so-called "double" centers are reproductive organs partially converted into the petals of double flowers, which protrude from the four large outside petals and shape up like a raspberry or thimble. These varieties are available:

'Bizarre'—Dark bronze leaves; pink flower petals with crested chartreuse center; small yellow petals inside.

'Cinderella'—Red-leaved thimble type with pink flowers sometimes streaked gold, or tipped cherry-red.

'Curly Locks'—Leaves, dark bronze; thimble, bright yellow; upper petals, pink.

'Fire Fly'—Crested flowers, coral-red; foliage, deep mahogany.

'Goldylocks'—Pink thimble flowers; dark red leaves.

'Perryann'—Dark red leaves; large pink thimble flowers.

'Pied Piper'—Dwarf with bronze foliage, light pink crested flowers.

'Pistachio'—Red foliage; flower petals pink; thimble, yellow-green.

'Robin Hood'—Bronze-leaved midget with red-eyed soft pink flowers.

'Stop Light'—Dark red leaves; dark red thimble with raised center in wine-red.

'Thimbleberry'—A group of dark-leaved varieties with pink or red flowers, or combinations such as red with gold crest.

DOUBLE-FLOWERING SEMPS

These fully double flowers, in all shades of white to red plus some bicolors, are called "rose," "rosebud," or "camellia" flowering begonias. They are slightly more difficult to grow to perfection than the single-flowering varieties. But the little dancing powder-puff balls with literally dozens of closely packed petals more than repay you for any extra effort involved.

For the most abundant and sizable double flowers, try to grow these beauties at 70° or under—but in fairly high humidity. The drier the air and the higher the temperature, the smaller and more sparse the bloom. It is also vital to pinch out young plants at least once, and to cut back severely after flowering. Without exception, stem cuttings should have at least one branch.

'Apple Blossom'—Pale pink double flowers; green leaves.

'Ballet'—Eye-catcher with dark red leaves, double white pompom flowers.

'Bo-Peep'—Dark foliage; dark pink flowers.

'Christmas Candle'—Green leaves; double holiday-red flowers.

'Dainty Maid'—Green leaves; white flowers tipped with pink.

'Depesne'—Green leaves; double pink flowers.

'Ernest K.'—Dark red leaves; rose-red rosebud flowers.

'Flame'—Bronzy leaves; scarlet flowers.

'Geneva'—A group with green leaves, double flowers in your choice of many shades of pink and red. Robust.

'Jack Horner'—Dark leaves; pink flowers.

'Joan Strong'—Bronze leaves; pink flowers.

'Little Gem'—Miniature with dark red leaves, rosy pink flowers. Grows slowly, stays small.

'Lucy Lockett'—Dark red leaves; bright pink blooms.

'Luscious'—Dark foliage; pink flowers shading to pearly white.

'Old Lace'—Bronze foliage; rose-pink flowers.

'Pink Camellia'—Good grower with dark red leaves, deep pink flowers.

'Pink Wonder'—Green leaves; pink flowers.

'Red Camellia'—Dark leaves; deep red flowers.

'Snowdrop'—Bronze-red leaves; white flowers. Dwarf.

'Snow White'—Green leaves; heavenly white flowers.

'Swanson's'—Choose pink or rose flowers on vigorous plants with dark red leaves.

'Weepy'—Maroon-red leaves; dark red flowers.

'Westport Beauty' (sometimes listed as 'Gustav Lind')—Green leaves; pink flowers. One of the original doubles.

'Winkie'—Compact, with dark foliage, old-rose flowers.

CALLA-LILY BEGONIAS

Legendarily, the only place these temperamental queens were happy was in an old-time New England farmhouse kitchen, where the air was coolish in winter and the teakettle steamed constantly on the coal stove. Of course, this isn't necessarily so today. We need only take our cue from the conditions in that kitchen, and reproduce them as nearly as possible.

"Cool" is a must for callas—65° by day, if possible, and slightly less at night. So is "dry"—they should never be watered unless the soil ball is completely dried out. Overwatering can cause rot almost before you set your watering can down. "Humid" is the secret of healthy, lively leaves and plentiful supply of flowers.

"Don't disturb" is another byword. Calla-lily begonias dislike moving from house to house, even from window to window. Settle them where they're happy, and let them stay there. Shade them from hot sun, which crisps and reddens leaves that should be white and fresh; but give them enough sun, particularly in the winter, to encourage flowering and to produce healthy, fresh green leaf color. Guard them against sudden or constant drafts, which can cause callas to fold up overnight.

Calla-lily begonias are not particularly finicky about soil mix, are not heavy feeders. Like other *semperflorens* begonias, they should be pruned back drastically after flowering.

Remember this about taking cuttings from callas. At least half the leaf area should have the green coloring of chlorophyll, or the shoot will probably not root. An all-white or near-white cutting can't carry on the life processes while roots are forming. Chances are, too, that these cuttings will need the extra humidity and protection of a prop box.

Unless you can provide the perfect calla-preferred growing conditions, look for the varieties with the largest and heaviest leaves and sturdiest stems. The thinner-leaved, more delicate plants are that much more difficult and demanding to grow.

But don't let anyone tell you that calla-lily begonias are impossible. Simply keep cool temperature and other cultural requirements in mind, and go ahead. This is one plant so heavenly, so rare, it's worth every bit of coddling it calls for.

Many growers simply offer "calla-lily begonias" with a note as to whether the flowers are red or pink, single or double. Among the named callas, the 'Maine Variety' is stronger, with heavier leaves and stems, single red flowers—a good bet for beginners. "Cherry Sundae' is a new, double-red-flowering calla that's also vigorous and less temperamental.

More ethereal and delicate are 'Pink Jewel,' semidouble pink; 'Ruby Jewel,' semidouble red; and 'Calla Queen,' single rose-red flowers.

Often classed as callas or calla-type begonias are two varieties with green leaves spotted and blotched with bright yellow, which are considerably less touchy about their cultural preferences. 'New Hampshire' has plenteous single pink flowers. 'Charm' is a chance seedling of a calla—also single pink flowers—with the charming habit of tinging its leopard-spotted leaves pink in good sunlight.

CHAPTER 7

Angel-Wing Begonias

Categorizing these personable begonias places one promptly " 'twixt the devil and the deep blue sea." Botanically, the group should be labeled "cane-stemmed begonias," and should include all those with bamboo-like stems and distantly spaced and swollen joints, or nodes. Popularly, most of these plants have been dubbed "angel-wing begonias," an aptly descriptive term for leaves with one lobe larger and higher than the other, at the stem end—dead ringers for angels' or doves' wings.

We're being devilish, and sticking with the popular terminology. Angel-wing begonias in this chapter have both wing-shaped leaves and bamboo-like stems. Other cane-stemmed varieties, and varieties with angel-wing leaves that are not cane-stemmed, have been classified according to such characteristics as hairy leaves, upright and branching growth, and the like.

Such scientific inconsistencies explained away, let's get rhapsodic about the angel-wing begonias. What beauties they are! Tall and statuesque, or small and delicately feminine. The winglike leaves may be as soft and lustrous as shimmering silk, or taffeta-sheer and crisp. Many are deep, glowing green accented with white, pink, or shining silver dots or splotches of all sizes. Some are smooth; others are many-pointed on the edge; some add feathery ruffling. The leaves may grow as long as eight inches, or stay under two.

And such spectacular flower clusters! From stem joints and tips, branching clusters drip down—sometimes so heavy with flowers that the boughs are weighed down with bloom. There may be as many as thirty blossoms in a single cluster—male, female, or both. And this gloriously colorful miracle may come to pass twice, thrice, or more, at intervals during the year. Look up, sometime, to a flowering angel-wing begonia in a basket overhead. You'll gasp at its beauty.

HOW TO GROW ANGEL-WING BEGONIAS

General begonia culture, as discussed in Chapter 3, suits these varieties very well. The soil mix may lean slightly toward the heavier side, but not necessarily. An extra ration of sunlight will increase flowering. Humidity does not need to be of the highest.

Careful watering is important. Don't water unless the soil in the pot has dried out completely. When an angel-wing begonia is kept too moist, it drops its apparently healthy lower leaves in quick succession, and repeatedly grows new ones from the same stem joints.

Judicious pruning is also important. Many angel-wings will gleefully grow up to three, four, five feet—even more. But in the process, the lower stems may become bare and ungainly, the remaining leaves forming a comical tassel at the top. Pruning keeps the size within reasonable limits and encourages growth of side shoots and bottom growth from the roots.

The finest and largest flowers are produced on young, green, vigorous growth. Pinch out young plants—seedlings or rooted cuttings —early in life. On mature plants, prune out hard, old, woody stems after each flowering, and in spring when new growth begins.

HOW TO PROPAGATE ANGEL-WING BEGONIAS

The angel-wings propagate easily from any of the methods described in Chapter 4, except leaf cuttings and layering. Divisions of older, well-branched plants at the base is safe and sure.

Seeds

Natural species of angel-wing begonias grow as readily from seeds as the *semperflorens* types. Also, some old-time hybrids have their characteristics so firmly entrenched that they will come fairly true from seed. Seedlings of either or both have an impish way of displaying, on their first tiny true leaves, delightfully conspicuous silver spots. Usually (but not always) this is a sign that the mature leaves will sport some sort of spots.

Stem Cuttings

Angel-wings will often make roots in a glass of water, without benefit of any special prop-box protection. If they are kept in a

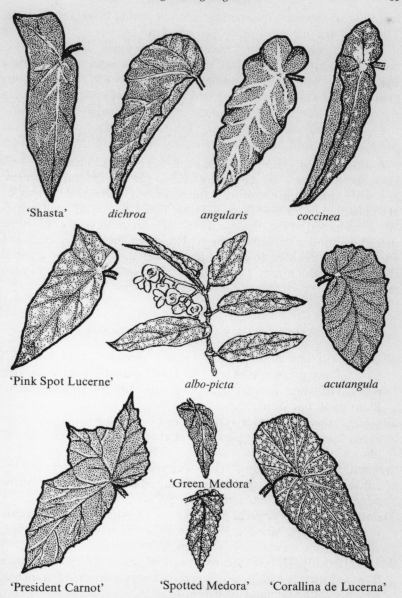

'Shasta'   *dichroa*   *angularis*   *coccinea*

'Pink Spot Lucerne'   *albo-picta*   *acutangula*

'Green Medora'

'President Carnot'   'Spotted Medora'   'Corallina de Lucerna'

ANGEL-WING BEGONIAS

humid area, however, the rooting medium should be on the dry side. The stems are juicy and subject to quick rot.

For a bushier, branching plant in double-quick time, plant several rooted cuttings in one pot—the tip of each stem turned toward the outside. Expect bloom soon, on this new growth. Don't be surprised if your cutting begins to bud even while it's rooting.

NAMED VARIETIES OF ANGEL-WING BEGONIAS

Rather than grouping these plants for beginners, advanced growers, and collectors—which might lead to the impression that there is a wide variation in culture—the following varietal descriptions are classified according to size. Those listed as "small" will generally keep under a foot; those called "tall" can go to six feet or more, in a greenhouse or a California garden. After these two groups is a short section devoted to desirable new varieties not yet in general distribution which may be available when or soon after you read this book.

SMALL ANGEL-WING BEGONIAS

albo-picta (variety of *maculata*)—Name means "painted white." Slim, glossy green leaves with sharply tapered points and silver spots. Off-white flowers drooping from tips of slender stems. Plant small but sturdy.

albo-picta rosea—A lustier variation of *albo-picta* with larger, plain green leaves and deep pink flower clusters. More showy in full bloom.

'Bennett' (*coccinea* seedling)—Few-branched plant grows bushy because it sends up many stems. Small, dark leaves wavy on the edge; flowers glowing salmon.

'Dainty Spray' (*alba perfecta grandiflora* x 'Di-Anna')—Impish dwarf in perfect scale. Slender, Kelly-green leaves with crinkled edge; clusters of delicate face-powder-pink flowers.

dichroa (Brazil)—Name means "two-colored." Brilliant orange-flowered species with five-inch green leaves on drooping branches. Resents chills; demands constant heat.

'Elaine' ('Lucerna' seedling)—Notable parent of glamorous 'Pinafore.' Narrow, rolling, red-lined leaves; flowers showy, rosy pink. Grows low.

'Jinnie May' (*coccinea* seedling)—With careful and constant pruning, plant stays delightfully small. Small green leaves crowd each other on well-branched stems. Bright red flowers off and on all year.

'Lawrence H. Fewkes'—Silver-dotted, medium green leaves; clear pink flowers in dangling clusters.

'Lobata Variegata'—Name means "lobed" and "variegated." White-flowered old-timer with silver-spotted leaves of ruffled green satin.

'Lugano' ('Lucerna' seedling)—Miniature with toothed leaves fleetingly silver-spotted; small flowers, lobster-pink.

'May Queen' (*albo-picta* seedling)—Small, shamrock-green leaves with silver polka dots; white flowers. Plant stays low, branches freely.

'Medora'—Originated in Medora, Illinois. Dwarf, branching plant in your choice of two patterns—pink flowers and flat, dark green foliage; or smooth, silver-sprinkled leaves and white flowers. Usually listed separately as 'Green Medora' and 'Medora.'

'Mrs. Schinkle' (*coccinea* seedling)—Tapering, slightly cupped green leaves; moderate-sized clusters of orchid-pink flowers.

'Mrs. W. A. Wallow'—Named for originator's wife. Wavy, wing-shaped leaves curl up on the edge; constant bountiful flowers in pink or white.

'Orange Rubra' (*dichroa* x 'Coral Rubra')—Clear green leaves sometimes faintly silver-spotted; sometimes not. Ornate clusters of large salmon-orange flowers outshine the foliage. Tidy, neat grower.

'Orrell' ('Lucerna' seedling)—Sturdy plant with ruffled, silver-spotted fresh green leaves, short clusters of cherry-red flowers.

'Perfectiflora'—Name means "perfect-flowered." Small, shield-shaped, bright green leaves, wavy margins; large white flowers. Stays small.

'Perle de Gard'—Bushy, freely branching, medium-sized plant with triangular green leaves lightly silver-spotted, cupped to show red lining beneath; large flowers glowing crimson.

'Pinafore' ('Elaine' seedling)—Slim, substantial, crimped-edged leaves dark slate-green with faint silver spots; beet-red beneath; bright salmon flowers, not large and gaudy, but long-lasting and plentiful. Unusual.

'Pink Spot Lucerne' ('Corallina de Lucerna' x *dichroa*)—Leaves of forest-green satin patterned with pink polka dots; large carmine flowers.

'Red Compta,' or 'Tewkesbury Red'—Low, slow grower with leaves tinged red over bronze, brilliant red beneath; flowers crimson. Not one of the easiest.

'Rosie Murphiski' ('Lucerna' seedling)—Delightful name for a lady-like plant with crinkly, silver-spotted green leaves, pink flowers.

'Sara-Belle' ('Maybelle E.' seedling)—Scarce but desirable plant with pleasant habit of sending up several canes from the roots. Leaves of watercress green, thickly and lastingly silver-spotted; underneath, reddish veins on jade-green flushed with purple; flowers pink to red.

'Spring Song'—Perky silver-spotted leaves; delicate pink flowers.

'Suretta' ('Lucerna' seedling)—Medium, bushy grower; lobed wing-shaped leaves, silver-spotted, bronzy green; flowers, white or palest pink.

'Veitch's Carmine' (*dregei* x *coccinea*)—Named for horticulturist Veitch. Pleasant, medium-sized plant with red-rimmed green leaves, brilliant clusters of carmine flowers.

TALL ANGEL-WING BEGONIAS

acutangula, or *acutangularis*—Name means "sharply angled stems." Lustrous, smooth, slightly pointed green leaves toothed and ruffled on the edge; pink-petaled male flowers like scallop shells, open to show rich golden centers. Unusual features—unfolding new leaves puckered and lined with bright red; fairly thick stems distinctly six-sided and grooved between. Habit, a bit bare and leggy below, but graceful and lovely above.

'Alma Milliken' ('Superba-Kenzi' seedling)—Matronly cane type with sturdy, straight stems up to five feet; silver-splashed leaves tinted red at the edge and underneath; dangling clusters of pink flowers.

'Alzasco' ('Lucerna' seedling)—Dark-complexioned plant with ruffled leaves nearly black, silver-spotted, except in strong light; somber maroon below; clustering female flowers, deep, brilliant red.

angularis, or *zebrina* (Brazil)—Name means "angular stems." Tall aristocratic species with long, oval-pointed leaves of gray-green silk moiré strikingly veined with pearl-gray, toothed and undulating on the edge; short-stemmed white flowers, not of the showiest.

'Annabelle'—Sturdy-stemmed variety with aspirations to height; well branched and well covered with Irish-green, silver-spotted leaves; generous flowers in soft cosmetic pink.

'Argentea-Guttata' (*albo-picta* x *olbia*)—Name means "silver-speckled." Nicknamed "trout leaf," for its resemblance to the skin of a lake trout. Stout and well branched; innumerable small silver spots on typically pointed olive-colored leaves, red-lined beneath. Cream-colored flowers sometimes tint pink in strong light. Also available: 'Red Argentea,' with scarlet flowers.

'Arlene' (*coccinea* seedling)—Bushy, upright grower with pointed, green, lance-shaped leaves lightly salted with silver, red below; flowers, white on the edge, gradually shading in to pink.

coccinea (Brazil)—Name means "scarlet." Bright green leaves unbroken by spots or splotches; pink- and red-flowering types available. Parent of many illustrious hybrids; will top fifteen feet.

compta—Name means "ornamented." Tall grower from Brazil; has large leaves of gray-green silk, strikingly striped along the veins with pearly silver; flowers white.

'Constance' ('Lucerna' seedling)—Lustrous bronze, pink-spotted leaves of medium size; boastful, pendant clusters of light red flowers, paler toward the center. May grow to six feet.

'Corallina de Lucerna' (*teuscheri* x *coccinea*)—First name means "coral-red"; last name honors Swiss lake. White-spotted green leaves and great, constant bunches of coral flowers. A giant, used for hedges in California. Prune savagely after flowering. Often listed simply as 'Lucerna.' One of the large angel-wings most frequently grown.

'Decorus'—Name means "comely" or "becoming." The same or a similar well-mannered plant is sold as 'Undulata.' Smooth green leaves undulate, or waved on the edge and between the veins; flowers, white.

'Di-Anna' (*dichroa* x 'Annie Laurie')—Long, narrow birds'-wing leaves thickly pleated and ruffled, silver-spotted. Salmon-pink flowers. To three feet tall.

'Di-Erna' (*dichroa* x *rubra*)—Slim, pointed green leaves; orange-red flowers. Grows to four feet or more. Blooms almost constantly if not overpotted.

'Di-Shasta' (*dichroa* x 'Shasta')—Similar to 'Di-Erna,' but taller. Large leaves smooth, even green, red-tinted on the back; flowers, scarlet.

'Elithe' (*coccinea* seedling)—Slim green leaves lightly silver-spotted, and red-backed; flowers, deep pink. Many stems and branches. To six feet tall.

'Elvira Swisher' (*aconitifolia* seedling)—Robust cane-stem with large, silky-satin leaves, dark green, faintly dusted with silver; flowers, lavender-pink.

'Grace' (*coccinea* seedling)—Typical, solid green angel-wing leaves; untypical white flowers centered with showy golden stamens.

'Grey Feather' (*compta* seedling)—Slim leaves, more gray than green, heavy and thickish, with distinct "feather" formed by cream-colored veins; blooms white with pink tinge. Branches freely.

'Helen'—Shimmering bronze-green leaves pointed on the edge, like 'President Carnot.' Pearly white flowers.

'Helen W. King' ('Lucerna' seedling)—Semitrailer with drooping branches, long-oval leaves bronze over green, and highlighted by circles of solid silver in odd sizes, red beneath; luscious pink flowers. Grows to five feet or more.

'Helena'—Large pale green leaves with ruffled edge; white flowers.

'Interlaken' ('Lucerna' seedling)—Eager grower must be pinched, kept within bounds, or will top six feet. Rich clusters of deep red flowers; wavy-edged leaves may have faint silver spots, may not.

'Kewensis'—Named for England's Kew Gardens. Spreading branches with modest, fluted, pointed green leaves; white flowers in tight, dipping clusters.

'Lucerna'—See 'Corallina de Lucerna.'

maculata (Brazil)—Name means "spotted." This was the first begonia found with silver-splotched foliage. Leaves lobed and toothed, dark, dull green; flowers, pink. The variety *wighti* has greenish-white flowers.

'Mme. de Lesseps' ('Argentea-Guttata' x *olbia*)—Tall, dark, handsome old-timer with indistinct silver spots, distinctively large clusters of white flowers. Often needs staking.

'Mrs. W. D. Harney' (*coccinea* seedling)—Long, smooth, fresh green leaves; pure white flowers; willing bloomer. Grows to ten feet or more.

'Noordi' ('Lucerna' x a *coccinea* variety)—Long, pointed-oval leaves of fresh, clean green; red flowers look orange in the sun.

'Picturatus' (seedling of *diadema* or *aconitifolia*)—Silver-patterned dark green leaves deeply cut and toothed, red on the edge and underneath; flowers, large, warm pink.

'Pink Parade' (*dichroa* seedling)—Wavy bronzed leaves thickly silver-spotted; shrimp-pink flowers.

'Pink Rubra'—Profusion of clear green, wing-shaped leaves, reddish-pink flowers. Strong grower has reached nine feet high, spreading fanlike over six feet.

'Pink Wave'—Green leaves with a permanent curl on the edge; prolific apricot-pink flowers. Upright if staked; graceful in a basket.

'President Carnot' (*olbia* x *coccinea* or 'Corallina de Lucerna')—Named for French President. Old-time favorite, still popular today. Prodigious grower with satiny, copper-green leaves crinkled and crisply pointed along the edge, sometimes silver-spotted, reddish below; flowers, red, carmine, or pink, depending on sun and light. Eager bloomer, even as a cutting.

'Ross Swisher' (*aconitifolia* seedling)—Named for grower's husband. Shimmering green leaves large and silver-spotted. Flowers, rosy pink.

'Rossi' ('Lucerna' seedling)—Tall but well-branched. Broad light green leaves tinged gold on the edge, haphazardly dotted with silver; fairy-like pink flowers.

'Rubaiyat' (*dichroa* seedling)—Lusty grower, bushy and many-stemmed; leaves gleaming green, occasionally dotted with silver; large clusters of soft pink flowers. Grows to four feet.

'Shasta' (*coccinea* seedling)—Handsome variety with long green leaves exaggeratedly wing-shaped; white flowers. 'Pink Shasta,' most often offered, has flowers of apple-blossom tints.

'Superba-Azella' (*aconitifolia* x 'Lucerna')—One of a group of robust 'Superba' hybrids with large, satiny, silver-marked leaves. This variety has pink flowers.

'Sylvan Delight'—Large, satiny, light green leaves; pink flowers. One of a group of 'Sylvan' hybrids.

'Sylvan Grandeur'—Silvery-pink dots all over heavy, lighter-veined green leaves, red underneath; flowers, pink.

undulata (Brazil)—Name means "ruffled." Shiny green leaves on spreading branches; tight clusters of white flowers. See 'Decorus.'

'Velma S.' (*coccinea* seedling)—Grass-green, concave leaves; flowers rosy-red.

'Winning Way'—Wavy, silver-speckled leaves; pink flowers.

VARIETIES TO WATCH OR WAIT FOR

'Anna Christine' ('Salmon Rubra' x *dichroa*)—Habit dwarf; leaves large, leathery-looking, mahogany over green; lightly waved edges. Flowers, deep, bright cerise. May be observed in Montreal's Botanical Gardens.

The 'Supremes'—A group of newly registered hybrids ('Shasta' x *dichroa*) of intermediate growth, leaves in various versions of the angel-wing. 'Rose Supreme' leaves are large, oblong, wavy; flowers, deep rose. 'Pink Supreme' leaves are wedge-shaped, green with silver spots, slightly red beneath; flowers, orchid-pink. 'Orange Supreme' leaves are smallish, oblong, smooth green; flowers, shrimp to orange. 'Scarlet Supreme' leaves are plain green, lance-shaped, smooth, and rather thick; flowers, deep pink to scarlet.

CHAPTER 8

Hairy-Leaved Begonias

The correct botanical term, here, is "hirsute." It applies to a group of begonias with hairy leaves and bewhiskered flowers. The hair may be as silky-fine and thick as in velvet, or as stiff, bristly, and widely spaced as in a brush. The same or similar hair is usually found along the stem, and on the outside of the flower petals.

In this group, as defined here, are hairy-leaved begonias which have a branching habit and upright, bushy growth. There are also rhizomatous varieties with hairy or fuzzy leaves (Chapter 11), and some hirsute types in the odd and rare class (Chapter 13).

A few of the all-time-favorite begonias, and many of the most rarely lovely, belong to this group. The effect of light shimmering over, or through, a leaf upholstered with millions of minute hairs is breathtaking. The short, long, or felted hairs may be the same color as the leaf surface, or in contrast. The leaves come in all shapes, from roundish, to finger-lobed, to tapering-pointed.

And the flowers! On them, a beard is a glamorous attribute. Sometimes the same color as the petals, more often striking red on pink, pink on white, or the like, these hairs lift the flowering plant right out of the ordinary class into the superb.

HOW TO GROW HAIRY-LEAVED BEGONIAS

This is another group that's easy to grow. The plants seem to wear their hairs like a coat, which protects them against drying out in drought times, getting cold feet if chilled, or shriveling up in dry air. Again, the all-important caution against too much water—rot is a disastrous result.

The more sunlight, except in hottest summer, the more likely your plant will flower, and bountifully. Don't expect bloom, however, until the plant is well established and fairly mature.

A number of hairy-leaved begonias can be induced to droop, and

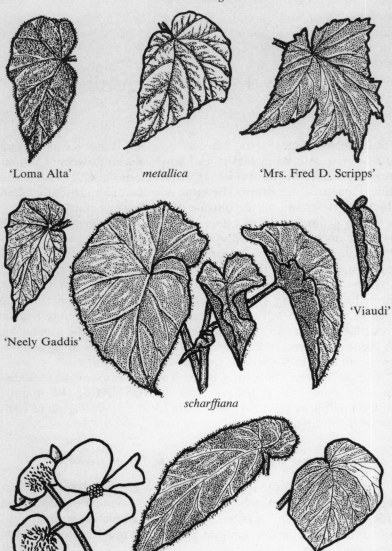

'Loma Alta'   *metallica*   'Mrs. Fred D. Scripps'

'Neely Gaddis'   'Viaudi'

scharffiana

Hairy Flowers   *macrocarpa pubescens*   *scabrida*

HAIRY-LEAVED BEGONIAS

are beautiful in baskets. Naturally, these should not be pinched out, but are allowed to grow and branch at will. When the branches are tall and top-heavy, let the soil stay dry until the plant is limp. Attach light weights, such as clothespins, to the ends of the main branches for a few days after watering, to hold them down.

HOW TO PROPAGATE HAIRY-LEAVED BEGONIAS

Leaf cuttings are not usually successful for these plants, but all other propagating methods in Chapter 4 except layering are easy and sure. Seeds of species and some old, inbred hybrids, will make new plants at a fairly rapid rate, and are grown slightly drier than other types.

Stem Cuttings

These too should be rooted somewhat on the dry side—usually in a prop box or some other protective device. If you find they have a tendency to rot before they root, try rubbing the hairs gently off the stems with your fingers. Occasionally these hairs seem to hold in rot-provoking moisture.

NAMED VARIETIES OF HAIRY-LEAVED BEGONIAS

Some of these begonias are widely grown and definitely easier to grow than others. These are included in the beginners' list. Others are fairly easy, with some special care—and are grouped under the heading "For Advanced Growers." Then there are the collectors' items, which may fall into that category because they are somewhat temperamental, or because they are somewhat hard to find. Finally are described varieties not known to be distributed for sale at this time, but that may be in the near future. They are gems to look forward to, worth waiting and hunting for.

FOR BEGINNERS

'Alleryi' (*metallica* x *gigantea*)—Named for French hybridizer Allery. Resembles its mother, but is easier to grow. Darker, tougher-looking bright green leaves, hoary-frosted and accented with deep purple veins, coarsely cut on the edge. Show-stopping pale pink flowers bewhiskered with silky-fine hairs in the fall. May have a tendency toward bare lower stems; pinch out when young.

'Alto Scharff' (*scharffiana* x *alto de serra*)—Combination name for both parents. Spreading, bushy, soft-looking plant of moderate height. White-fuzzed green leaves, red underneath, with red hair tipping each short point on the edge. Stems arch proudly. Two-toned white and pink flowers thinly edged with red; buds bristle with red hairs. Good basket subject.

'Cypraea' (*metallica* seedling)—Name means "copper-colored." Moderate-sized, well-branched variety with dark-veined green leaves, pink-haired white flowers.

'Drosti' (*scharffi* seedling or variety)—Heavy leaves so hairy that they seem in a cloud or fog, distinguished by deep purple lining beneath; red-bearded petals on pink flowers. Grows larger than its parent.

'Houghtoni' (*scharffiana* seedling)—Named for begonia authority, Dr. Houghton. The dwarf form it most frequently sold, and most adaptable to window-sill growing. Looks like a low, full, bushy *scharffi*—leaves of tawny plush, heavy-drooping bouquets of pink-bearded flowers. Effective in baskets.

'Mrs. Fred D. Scripps' (*scharffiana* x *luxurians*)—Beige-green hairy leaves deeply divided into long, pointed scallops, often with a small extra "finger" standing up at the top where stem ends; underside, red. Small white star flowers cluster and droop daintily in early spring. A distinctive beauty; good bet for a flower-show prize.

'Nelly Bly' ('Cypraea' seedling)—Named for the song. Bushy and branching, with dark green leaves, red underneath. Red-bearded pink flowers.

'Prunifolia' ('Viaudi' seedling)—Thick, cupped leaves of darkest olive-green flushed dull red beneath—distinctive, sparse white hairs over all. White flowers with stiff, spiny beard.

scharffi, or *haageana* (Brazil)—Named for co-discoverer Scharff. This is the great-great-granddaddy of many of today's velvety beauties, still widely known, grown, and loved. Large leaves point downward, shimmer under a coat of silky white hairs over olive-green; red below. Monstrously heavy clusters of large white flowers with delightful pink beards.

ANGEL-WING BEGONIAS

TOP ROW: 'Veitch's Carmine,' 'Grey Feather,' 'Orange Rubra.' MIDDLE ROW: 'President Carnot,' 'Pinafore.' BOTTOM ROW: 'Di-Erna,' *coccinea,* 'Argentea–Guttata.'

FOR ADVANCED GROWERS

'Conbow' ('Thurstoni' seedling)—Wide-oval, fuzzy green leaves, somewhat cupped; red below; bearded pink flowers.

'Credneri' (*scharffiana* x *metallica*)—Sometimes called 'Hairy Thurstoni'—also resembles *sanguinea* with a white beard. Leaves thick, often cupped or the opposite. Pink whiskers on pink flowers.

'd'Artagnon.' See Basket Begonias, page 119.

'Druryi' ('Cypraea' x *sanguinea*)—Large leaves, darkest green of the silk-hairy type, red-lined. Flowers white with red beard.

'Duchartrei' (*echinosepala* x *scharffiana*)—Moderate-sized, white-hairy, leaves green over and under, with red veins; white flowers boast thick pink beards.

fernando-costae—Named for a friend of the collector. Eye-stopping plant with fleshy green, cupped, roundish leaves; inconspicuous hairs; white flowers. Tendency to trail; might be good in baskets. Will grow slightly more moist.

macrocarpa pubescens—Variety of the African species *macrocarpa*, with tapering leaves soft and silky as finest camel's hair—subdued green on top, usually cupped to reveal ruby lining underneath, and jewel-like when light shines through. Similar to *laeteviridea,* but slightly less delicate. The real difference is in technical flower characteristics.

'Margaritae' (*echinosepala* x *metallica*)—Branching bush with dull green, smallish leaves darker at the veins, enlivened by a coat of lustrous white hairs. Pink flowers with conspicuous red whiskers. Should not be confused with 'Margaritacea,' with metallic-purple leaves.

metallica (Brazil)—Small leaves cut and pointed, glistening silver hairs over dark green, indented purple veins. Pink flowers have show-off red bristles. Stem cuttings root best when almost bone-dry.

'Rufida' ('Viaudi' x 'Prunifolia')—Five-inch bronzy-green leaves, wine-red beneath, densely hairy all over. Large pink flowers with scarlet whiskers. Grows big and bushy.

scharffiana (Brazil)—Named for co-discoverer Scharff. Best described by comparison with better-known *scharffi.* Somewhat smaller; less prominent veins; more pronounced "tail" on reversible green-red plush leaves; lobes overlap at stem end. Red whiskers on ivory flowers. Less rigid branches make this a beauty in a basket.

subvillosa (Brazil)—Name means "shaggy," "soft-hairy." Sometimes listed as *scotch luxurians.* Velvety, oval leaves, green over and under; stems juicy; flowers, white or pink. Does not branch frequently.

'Vedderi'—Named for its originator. Only one of two dissimilar begonias with a similar name seems to be available now. Tall type with pointed leaves of soft olive velvet; red beneath. Pink-bearded flowers.

'Viaudi' ('Duchartrei' x 'Pictaviensis')—Pointed two-by-five-inch leaves crisp as if starched, dull green on top, red below; over-all fine white-hairy. Bearded white flowers. Will grow to three feet or more.

FOR COLLECTORS

bradei (Brazil)—Species newly introduced, with dainty, slim, soft-hairy green leaves lined with red.

'Chiala'—Will grow into a three-foot bush. Lance-shaped leaves somewhat hairy, green above, and red beneath. White flowers with white beard. 'Rosea' variety has pink-bearded flowers.

'Clementa' (*scharffi* seedling)—Similar to its parent, with longer, greener leaves.

'Duscharf' ('Duchartrei' x *scharffiana*)—A more glamorous type of *scharffi* with brighter, broader leaves completely white-hairy; huge pink-whiskered white flowers.

echinosepala (Brazil)—Name means "prickly," or "spiny." This name has been given to a small *metallica*-like begonia, but properly belongs to a plant with regular, narrow, serrate leaves, not heavily haired, drooping from arched branches. Male flowers are white-bearded.

engleri (Africa)—Named for collector Engler. Curious plant with curly red-haired stems; dark green leaves with white hairs; pink flowers with red ovaries and hair.

'Frondosa' (*scharffi* seedling)—Name means "strong-growing." Branching, upright type with green leaves hoary with white silk; flowers, pink.

Hairy-leaved begonias: TOP ROW: *fernando-costae,* 'Mrs. Fred D. Scripps.' MIDDLE ROW: 'Drosti,' *macrocarpa pubescens,* 'Alleryi.' BOTTOM ROW: *scharffi,* 'Credneri.'

'Lady Clare' (*scharffiana* x *luxurians*)—Graceful, poised plant with soft-hairy ladyfingered leaves more beige than green; white flowers. New.

'Lady Vi' (*laeteviridea* x 'Viaudi')—Soft-hairy leaves light green on top, red underneath; bearded flowers; a rugged grower. New, not widely available yet.

laeteviridea (Africa)—Name means "light" or "bright green." Well-branched dwarf resembles *macrocarpa pubescens* except for flower characteristics. A stunning ball gown could be made of this green-wine reversible velvet. Flowers white.

'Loma Alta' (*scharffiana* seedling)—Rapid grower with thick, foot-long leaves, dark green on top, beet-red underneath. Rose-whiskered white flowers. Profuse bloomer; can go from cutting to five feet the first year. New.

'Neely Gaddis' ('Viaudi' seedling)—Named for grower's cousin. More angelic-looking than an angel-wing—green dove-wing leaves softened by white down; celestial white flowers with silky white hairs and golden stamens. 'Pink Neely Gaddis' has pink flowers, red-lined leaves.

'Richland'—Apple-green leaves, red stems, pink-hairy white flowers.

roxburghi (Himalayas)—Medium-sized, medium-green leaves, heart-shaped, with sawtooth edges, covered with small raised dots and fine white hairs; fragrant white flowers.

'San Miguel' (*venosa* x *scharffiana*)—Upright grower inherits papery stipules from *venosa*. Sturdy, with reddish brown stalks; new leaves, green; mature leaves, white-furred green with red backing. Small white flowers. New.

scabrida (Venezuela)—Name means "rough." Bright green, pointed-oval leaves, bristly rather than velvety; stout stems branch willingly; bridal showers of small white flowers in spring. Will grow to three feet or more.

'Vesperia' ('Viaudi' seedling)—Like a larger, fuller 'Margaritae'—brittle, hairy green leaves; pink-bearded, long-petaled white flowers.

'Viau-Scharff' ('Viaudi' x *scharffiana*)—Large, dark green leaves, purple beneath; ivory-bearded flowers.

'Zuensis' (*paulensis* x 'Credneri')—Firm, puckered green leaves in varying shapes and sizes; reddish, depressed veins; new leaves, soft and red-plushy; hairy flowers, deep pink. New.

VARIETIES TO WATCH OR WAIT FOR

hugelli (Brazil)—Named for Hugel. Broad, one-sided olive-green leaves; red underneath; white beard on white flowers.

'Leora' (*imperialis* x *metallica*)—Exciting new hybrid, not yet in distribution.

'Lillian Sloan' (*fernando-costae* x *metallica*)—New; not yet available.

'Ramirez' (*laeteviridea* seedling)—A variety of 'Alto Scharff'. Strong, dense grower with soft, velvety leaves lined with red.

CHAPTER 9

Other Upright, Branching Begonias

This is a motley assembly of plants, fascinating for that very reason. Their erect, bushy growth habit—and the fact that they are not properly angel-wing, hairy-leaved, *semperflorens,* or odd and rare begonias—are their only common characteristics. Otherwise, they are blessed by incredible variety.

For such a conglomerate group, pat cultural rules are hard to come by. If the general suggestions in Chapter 3 don't give you good results, study up on your particular plant. Perhaps your supplier can give you the clue to success. Or perhaps the varietal notes in this chapter may be of help.

Since they are upright and branching plants, it's fairly safe to suggest that most varieties will take—and like—pinching out tip growth from time to time, to create more compact shape.

Natural species can be grown, of course, from seeds. Stem cuttings—not leaves—are good propagating bets, usually with prop box or other protection during the rooting process.

NAMED VARIETIES—OTHER UPRIGHT, BRANCHING BEGONIAS

Varieties of easiest culture and most widespread availability are listed for beginners; slightly more difficult plants are grouped for advanced growers; and the more rare and temperamental, for collectors. Also described are items not now available but worth waiting or hunting for.

FOR BEGINNERS

'Braemar' (*scharffi* x *metallica*)—Named for the estate where it originated. Has been described as "*scharffiana* without a fur coat." Turtle-tailed, roundish leaves, glossy, thick, and cupped; over-all color effect, red-bronze. Branches and spreads readily, nice in baskets. Vigorous—cut back and restart if it outgrows its allotted space.

'Corbeille de Feu' (*semperflorens rubra* x *fuchsioides*)—Name is French for "basket of fire." Flaming red blossoms daintily tip the stems almost all year. Self-branching; needs no pinching. Wavy, perfect-oval leaves of waxy green precision.

'Dancing Girl'—Gives an angel-wing impression, but on inspection reveals that no two leaves are alike in shape, contour, size. Some are green with sparse silver spots; others, almost completely covered with silver. Silver dots may be arranged in a regular pattern, or hit or miss. Edges may be fluted, crinkled, pointed, plain. A carefree plant which shapes itself into buxom curves. Flowers, modest white.

'Frieda Grant'—Half-moon-shaped leaves, waxy olive-green, red beneath, densely covering the stems; small flowers, pinky-white.

incarnata (Mexico)—Name means "flesh-colored." Frilly, fluffy-looking plant with light green leaves charmingly fluted and scalloped on the edge; flesh-pink flowers in winter. Most ladylike and shapely when started from new cuttings each year.

'Mme. Fanny Giron' (*incarnata* x tuberous)—Christmas-hued plant with arching, drooping habit; clear, clean green leaves; large single scarlet flowers in frequent abundance.

odorata (South America)—Name means "scented." Bushier, lower-growing than *nitida;* similar patent-leather leaves slightly cupped when young. 'Odorata Alba' is a hybrid or seedling with white flowers with lily-like fragrance; *odorata rosea* has pink flowers. Both become awkward unless pinched before flower buds appear.

'Preussen' (German seedling)—Name means "Prussian." Generous supply of small, pointed, bronzy leaves spotted lightly with silver when mature: One of the most generous year-round bloomers, in delicate pink.

'Sachsen' (German seedling)—Sometimes listed as 'Saxony.' Slender, smooth, bronze-green leaves overlapping like feathers around a medium, much-branched plant. Featured attraction: bright red flowers off and on all year.

schmidtiana (Brazil)—Named for nurseryman Schmidt. Constantly branching plant, with small, hairy, green leaves, red-lined at the indented veins, red below. Continual supply of small, pale pink flowers. Sets seed easily. Delightful in baskets.

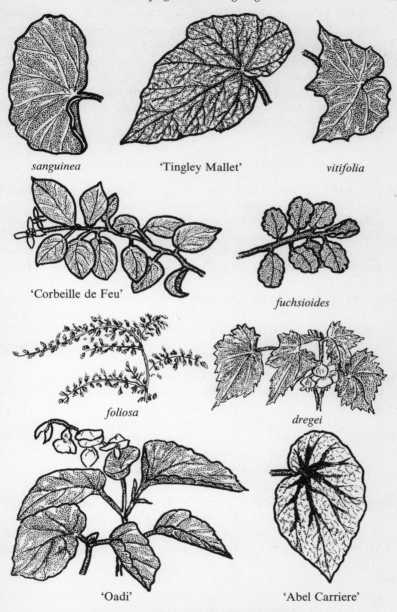

sanguinea   'Tingley Mallet'   *vitifolia*

'Corbeille de Feu'   *fuchsioides*

foliosa   *dregei*

'Oadi'   'Abel Carriere'

OTHER UPRIGHT, BRANCHING BEGONIAS

'Tea Rose' ('Odorata Alba' x *dichroa*)—Waxy, fresh green leaves;
fragrant light pink flowers. Will keep compact if pinched regularly.
'Thurstoni' (*metallica* x *sanguinea*)—Named for hybridizer Thurston.
Old favorite in New England barber- and tailorshops. Metallic
bronze-on-green leaves, highly polished, lined underneath with
scarlet; glossiest and most deeply colored with little sun. Hairy
flowers have been compared to "cerise chenille balls." Pinch out
to encourage branching.

FOR ADVANCED GROWERS

'Abel Carriere' (a rex variety x *evansiana*)—Changeable taffeta leaves,
silver with heavily marked green veins, rose-flushed in sun; underside, green with claret veins. Spasmodic sprays of rosy-pink
flowers throughout the year. This is a rex derivative, medium tall,
with erect and branching habit—has stems instead of rhizomes.
Leaves will burn and crisp in hot sun or dry air. Leaf cuttings
root readily.

'Catalina' ('Digswelliana' seedling)—Also called 'Lady Waterlow.'
Low, spreading plant with small green leaves and large flowers,
white inside, rosy outside; leaves and flowers color more intensely
with sun. Good winter bloomer; tolerates all but the hottest
summer sun.

cubensis (Cuba)—Also listed as: Cuban species, Cuban holly, holly-
leaf begonia. Crisply cut, shiny leaves, darkest green—a direct
take-off on holly, if slightly more crinkled. Snowy flowers in
winter. Droops and branches nicely in baskets.

'Digswelliana' (*fuchsioides* x *semperflorens*)—Freely branching winter-
bloomer (bright red) with fresh green leaves that crinkle up in cold
air. Heart-shaped male flower buds seldom open, look like tiny
valentines.

foliosa (Colombia)—Name means "full of leaves." Smallest-leaved
of all; often called the "fern begonia." Precise little green canoe-
shaped leaves alternate on each side of slender, drooping stems.
Midget bleeding-heart flowers. Keep warm, moist, humid. An
"Indian" variety is offered, with larger leaves.

'Frutescaria' (*fruticosa* seedling)—Like a more upright 'Frutescans'—
leaves somewhat lighter green, more deeply grooved by veins.
Sparse white flowers. Good in baskets.

Other upright, branching begonias: TOP ROW: *nitida, schmidtiana,* 'Mme. Fanny Giron.' MIDDLE ROW: 'Tea Rose,' 'Margaritaceae,' 'Catalina.' BOTTOM ROW: 'Corbeille de Feu,' 'Thurstoni,' *dregei.*

fuchsioides (Colombia; Mexico)—"Fuchsia-flowered" begonia, like a slightly larger *foliosa*. Identical, pointed, green ellipse-like leaves; clear pink drooping flowers. The *multiflora* variety is somewhat easier to grow and propagate. Variety *floribunda*, or *multiflora rosea*, is even larger, easier, more floriferous, with red blooms at branch tips.

'Ingrami' (*nitida* x *fuchsioides*)—Named for English grower Ingram. Slim green leaves with toothed edge; deep pink flowers. A full and bushy plant. Blooms best and most continually when grown cool, with plentiful sun.

'It' (*socotrana* x rex)—Bushy, rex-like dwarf prized for both foliage and multitudes of large light pink flowers. Cheerful, roundish leaves are light green, over-all splotched with silver. Beautifully branched; never straggles. Takes and likes more sun than rexes. Propagates freely by leaf or stem-tip cuttings.

kellermanni (Guatemala)—Deeply cupped green leaves, thick and completely covered with sheer white felt; angel-wing-like clusters of white flowers in late winter, early spring. Mature plant takes staking. To propagate, take stem cuttings after bloom; easy from seed.

'Margaritacea' ('Arthur Mallet' x 'Gloire de Sceaux')—Sturdier than the 'Mallet' type, with thicker leaves, characteristically purple-red overlaid with silver; free-blooming harmonious pink. No relation to hairy-leaved 'Margaritae.'

nitida (Jamaica)—Name means "shining." Often offered as *nitida alba*. Polished green leaves; china-white flowers. Needs pinching to keep plant in bounds. The begonia listed as *nitida odorata* is probably fragrant 'Odorata Alba'; *nitida rosea* is *odorata rosea*.

'Oadi' ('Odorata Alba' x *dichroa*)—Smooth, well-waved, grassy green leaves and stems look succulent, resemble the *semperflorens*, but have pointed tips. Large light pink flowers. Requires pinching.

'Richmondensis' ('Digswelliana' seedling)—Strong, succulent-looking plant; needs pinching to keep it shapely. Depending on sun and light, leaves vary from waxy light green to red-tinged, flowers from pink to red. Blooms all year under glass. Beautiful in a basket.

'Rogeri'—Smooth, shiny, bronzy-red leaves; resembles 'Thurstoni' but is smaller, more compact.

'Rosea-Gigantea' (*semperflorens* x *roezli*)—Large, juicy, *semperflorens*-shaped leaves with bright red spot at stem end, sometimes red-

rimmed. Long-lasting coral-red flowers in winter. Bushy but big.
sceptrum, or *aconitifolia* (Brazil)—Names mean "scepter-like" and
"resembling the aconite, or monkshood." Silky, dark green leaves
with sunken veins, cut deeply to separate the points, then cut
again to branch like antlers; irregularly and faintly silver-spotted.
Actually these are two distinct species, the latter the laciest-
looking; but either may be offered under either name.
vitifolia, or *lobulata* (Mexico)—Names mean "grape-leaved" or
"lobed." Plant branches from the base. Large, gleaming green
leaves finely toothed on the edge, somewhat downy beneath.
Flowers pink and white.
'Washington Street'—Imitates the peach leaf with shiny green,
toothed foliage on arched and branching stems; white flowers.
Rests in winter.

FOR COLLECTORS

alnifolia (Colombia)—Name means "leaves like the alder." Pointed-
oval leaves on woody stems, tipped with clusters of white flowers.
andina (Bolivia)—Name means "of the Andes." Heavyish light green
leaves covered with matted brown hairs; modest white flowers on
drooping branches; stems slender, tender.
'Anita Roseanna'—Bronze-red foliage; dark red flowers. Said to be
very free-flowering.
'Arabelle' ('Margaritacea' x 'Lulu Bower')—New "foliage" angel-
wing type with the metallic iridescence of the 'Mallet' begonias.
Thin, slender, purple-green leaves, with purple hair in each silver
spot; edge finely etched with silver; oxblood-red on the back;
veins, nearly black. Flowers pink.
'Arthur Mallet' (rex 'Eldorado' x *subpeltata*)—Small, branching shrub
with lightly hairy, metallic-purple leaves lined with dark veins,
which set off the large, clean, pink flower clusters. Rather demanding of warmth and high humidity. Leaf cuttings root in March or
April; stem cuttings at any time except winter.
'Axel Lange'—Named for the director of the Copenhagen Botanical
Gardens. Prefers growing up to out. Bronzy, medium-sized leaves
fade to light green at the edge; over-all sprinkled with silver;
bright russet underneath. Often listed with the rexes.
barkeri (Mexico)—Named for the discoverers' patron, Barker. Stiff,

military-mannered stems support bright green leaves with reddish edges in varying forms and shapes. Entire plant wears a blanket of woolly brown scurf. Winter-flowering; showy pink. Outdoor-grown in California, a monstrous specimen.

carpinifolia (Costa Rica)—Name means "like the blue beech." Branching miniature tree with slim, bristly green leaves that appear to be pleated.

'Dawn' ('Abel Carriere' seedling)—Dense little bush with pert, slim-pointed, dark green leaves with small, irregular silver freckles. Demands warmth and humidity.

'Decker's Select'—Many branching stems from the base keep the plant compact and shapely. Small, glossy green leaves sometimes blush at the edge. Flower buds like rosy hearts, open with petals of two shades of pink. Good bloomer.

'Dorothy Grant' ('Thurstoni' seedling)—Tall and vigorous, with polished bronze-green leaves cupped to reveal red lining beneath. Shy bloomer; white. Strong sun may fade leaf coloring.

'Gloire de Jouy'—A 'Mallet-type' begonia with metallic-bronze-over-green leaves lightly silver-sprinkled; flowers, blush-pink.

'Hattie Warden' (*sanguinea* seedling)—Thick, cupped leaves, olive-green on top, faced with deep red below. Large, heavenly white flowers, some with red hairs.

hirtella (Brazil)—Name means "somewhat hairy." Coarse, weedy plant with inconspicuous white flowers. Sets seeds freely.

involucrata (Costa Rica)—Name refers to the ring of bracts, or "involucre" around the flowers. Oval green leaves of fine velvet are divided by depressed veins. Many branches and new shoots from the base keep the plant bushy. Unusually tight clusters of white flowers. Leaves will brown and dry up in too-hot sun. Keep soil dryish.

isoptera (Java)—Name means "equal-winged." Compact plant with small, green, red-rimmed leaves, minute white flowers. Variety *hirsuta* has hairy leaves.

johnstoni (Africa)—Named for collector Johnston. Tall, loosely branched, with pale green leaves and red-spotted stems; few but large pink flowers.

longibarbata (Brazil)—Well-branched miniature bush with a succulent look. Heart-shaped leaves waxy green, scalloped on the edge. Flowers, white to pink. Easy from seed.

'Melisse' ('Margaritacea' x 'Lulu Bower')—Narrow leaf is pebble-textured, like the 'Mallet' types, but colored basic dark green with silver stippling. New.

'Red Kimball' (*dipetala* x *evansiana*)—Closely resembles *evansiana* with round, red-marked green leaves and red flowers, but not garden-hardy.

roezli (Peru)—Named for discoverer Roezl. Tall, rangy brancher with waxy green leaves, ruffled on the edge; pink flowers. Likes more sun than the average.

'Society' or 'Coriacea' (German seedling)—Short-stemmed, thick, cupped leaves, gleaming green on top, brown-felted beneath. Thin, papery, brown stipules. Flowers, white.

'Tingley Mallet' or 'Mme. Lionnet' (rex 'Edorado' x *subpeltata*)—Well-branched plant with characteristic 'Mallet' silver-on-purple leaves, brighter and sturdier. Easier to grow than brother 'Arthur.' Heavenly pink flowers off and on all year.

tomentosa (Brazil)—Name means "woolly." Thick, juicy leaves of rich green with downy hair beneath. Pink-rimmed white flowers with short red whiskers.

'Undine' ('Odorata Alba' seedling)—Lower, more shapely than its parent. Green leaves somewhat crinkled and channeled; pink- and white-shaded flowers often fragrant.

VARIETIES TO WATCH OR WAIT FOR

acuminata (Jamaica)—Name means "narrow, pointed." Crisply dainty plant dripping prim white flowers from arching stems; glossy, soft green leaves crinkled on the edge. Observed at Montreal Botanical Gardens.

'Bert Slatter' (*incarnata* x *kenworthyi*)—Named for former President of the American Begonia Society. Thin, large (six-by-ten) heart leaves, green overlaid with copper, toothed—the teeth tipped with red hair. Pink flowers almost all year. Bushy grower. New.

decandra (Mexico)—Small, well-branched plant with small, short-stemmed leaves; flowers, pinkish.

'Houston' (*incarnata sandersi* x *42S* seedling)—Medium, bushy plant; leaves, bronze-green faced with oxblood-red; pink flowers in summer.

pruinata (Costa Rica)—Name means "with powdery bloom." Smooth, rounded leaves glisten as if thinly iced with silver.

serratipetala (New Guinea)—Name means "serrated petals." Appealing, full-branched plant with slim, shiny leaves sharply cut and crinkled, spotted with raised pink dots. Female flowers have red-toothed petals.

ulmifolia (India)—Name means "elm-leaved." Tall grower favored for its oddity rather than beauty. Imitates the elm in leaf shape and color, with added rough hairs. Small white flowers.

SEMITUBEROUS "MAPLE-LEAF" BEGONIAS

This is a small group of upright, branching plants—some species, some hybrids—with leaves so like the maple, it's a "steal." They are semituberous in nature, but have no period of complete dormancy. This tuberous tendency often shows up in the way the stem swells up at, or immediately under, the soil level. Fairy-like are the smaller species, with leaves no larger than your little-finger nail. More robust are the larger-leaved hybrids from semituberous or tuberous begonias.

Culture depends on the delicacy of the variety you choose to grow. Generally, the species are more touchy, the hybrids more responsive to a minimum of care. All the good cultural conditions in Chapter 3 are called for, with little or no adaptation.

Occasionally these plants do not pull out of their winter resting period—which is not full dormancy, but a definite slowing down and even standing still. This is more likely with older plants than with young ones. When your plant shows signs of getting ready to rest, tip cuttings are wise insurance. A "heel" of semihard, woody stem taken with the leaf stem helps make sure that your cutting will root.

If you grow the semituberous species from seed, don't be surprised if the young leaves are silver-speckled, even up to the time the plants are nearly mature. You haven't found an exciting, illegitimate offspring. This is a frequent and delightfully natural phenomenon.

NAMED VARIETIES OF MAPLE-LEAF BEGONIAS

Actually, these plants are distinctly different from any other group of begonias. But the varieties are too few to merit a chapter of their own.

dregei (Africa)—Named for discoverer Drege. The true species' leaves are purple-veined on bronze, red underneath; but there are several acceptable variations and seedlings. Flowers are white. Grow warm and humid. This is the largest-leaved of the three original maple-leaf species, still thumbnail-size.

macbethi (Africa)—A *dregei* variation with smaller leaves, green veins. Variety *obtusa* leaves have blunter points; growth is more compact.

'Marie B. Holley'—A hybrid with fresh green, deeply cut, shiny leaves; porcelain-white flowers. Sturdier than the species, but must be kept shapely by pruning and pinching.

natalensis (Africa)—Named for Natal. Larger, less glamorous species with light-veined green leaves, white flowers.

'Richard Robinson' (*macbethi* seedling)—Cut-leaf-maple leaves colored silver over green, with red-brown veins, topped in winter by a snowy blanket of white flowers. Drops all its leaves and rests after flowering; keep warm and dry until new growth appears.

richardsiana (Africa)—Named for grower Richards. Lacy-looking dwarf with finest-cut maple leaves; flowers, white to pale pink.

'Weltoniensis' (*sutherlandi* x *dregei*)—Larger, all-green leaf with purplish veins; pink flowers. Variety 'Alba' blooms white.

CHAPTER 10

Basket Begonias

No matter what it's grown in—coffee tin, butter tub, clay pot, jardiniere—a well-grown begonia (or any other plant) is a sight that brightens your outlook on life. But take the same plant, put it in a basket, hang it slightly above eye level, and see how much more exciting it can be. There's something about looking up at it that adds new glamour.

And hanging baskets are such good decorators—airy, graceful, harmonizing with any motif or color scheme. For some reason, nature's colors seldom clash with each other, or with ours. And she contrives her plants' habits so that they enhance a well-designed container, camouflage a poor one.

There's no end to the number of begonias suitable for hanging baskets. Those described in this chapter are merely a sample. *Semper-florens* begonias are also blissfully happy in baskets, particularly when they've grown so big they're getting sprawly. The angel-wings droop naturally over the sides of a basket, and their dangling clusters of gorgeous flowers show off to greater advantage. Most of the rhizomatous varieties—and particularly those that creep and crawl on top of the soil—are extremely effective in hanging baskets. And of course, there are the pendant summer-blooming tuberous begonias, perhaps the most glorious and riotous of all.

The fact is, most begonias heartily appreciate the warmth and fresh air circulating around their pots, when they're hung high on the wall or in the window. This is good medicine for an ailing plant—a tender, delicate subject for which every other cultural cure has failed. And obviously, hanging baskets are space-savers. They need no spot on window sill or greenhouse bench.

The type of container depends largely on your personal taste and decorative objective, or the particular begonia you plan to grow in it. "Baskets" of plastic, ceramic, redwood, reed, metal, and many other materials are available in all sizes, shapes, and colors. Generally, the

115

less ornate the design, the better your plant shows off to advantage. Also note, when you buy a basket, whether or not it has drainage holes in the bottom. If it does, you will have to take care in watering that you don't wet anything below—or rig up some sort of saucer to catch the excess. If the basket has no bottom holes, you will want to put in at least two inches of sand, gravel, or other drainage material before you add soil mix. Or simply set the plant's pot on drainage material inside the basket.

Culturally, the best baskets are still those made of wire, lined with wood moss, or long-fibered sphagnum, and filled with light, porous soil mix. In these, plants' roots can breathe better. The moss holds moisture, but not too much. Lacking moss, I once lined a basket with a layer of wood ferns, and found it worked equally well. Of course, these baskets are best watered at the sink, where they can drip at will.

For something new and different, try combining two or more varieties of begonia in one large, shallow basket. In the center, plant an erect—but low-growing—variety, such as a waxy, bushy *semperflorens;* around the edge, a drooping trailer (*B. schmidtiana* grows happily this way). Or combine a large-leaved angel-wing ('Pinafore' or 'Orange Rubra') with a delicate, smaller variety ('Dainty Spray' or 'Medora'). Combine hairy-leaved 'Dwarf Houghtoni' with waxy-leaved 'Corbeille de Feu.' Or combine begonias with other plants— ferns, for example—for unusual effect. Only one caution: make sure all the plants in one basket have identical preferences as to soil, light, moisture, and other cultural considerations.

HOW TO GROW BASKET BEGONIAS

Here we have a matter of plants' individual preferences. These begonias are grouped together because of their trailing and hanging habits, not because of similar botanical characteristics and culture. Some like to grow moist, some should be kept on the dry side; some like lots of sun, some abhor it; some will tolerate dry air, some require high humidity. Specific cultural hints will be found with the varietal descriptions in this chapter.

Most trailing and hanging begonias branch and fill out better when the growing tips are pinched out from time to time, except immediately before flowering. On some plants, as they grow older, the stems will start to look bare and straggly; simply root some cuttings for a

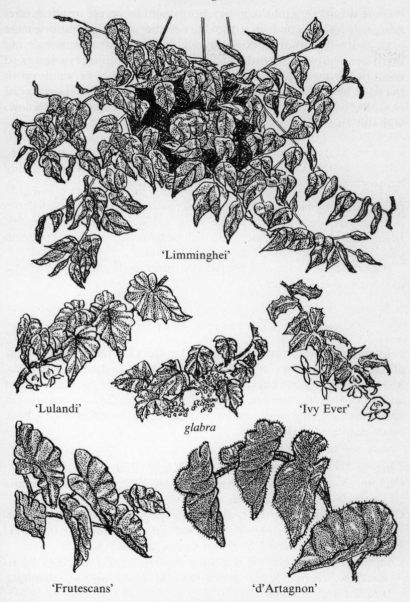

'Limminghei'

'Lulandi'

glabra

'Ivy Ever'

'Frutescans'

'd'Artagnon'

BASKET BEGONIAS

fresh new basket. All basket varieties benefit by severe pruning, after flowering has finished or at the start of the spring growing season.

Occasionally a basket begonia will develop a subborn streak and insist on climbing instead of hanging. You can quickly change its mind by letting it get so dry, it's limp. Then weight or gently tie down the ends of the branches for a few days, after watering. Hanging the basket above a window for a while, so the light comes from below, will also encourage trailers.

HOW TO PROPAGATE BASKET BEGONIAS

Most of these varieties take kindly and readily to safe-and-sure propagation by layering. Pin down stems at the joint (with a hairpin or bent wire) onto the soil in the same pot, or a smaller pot nearby. In an amazingly quick time, roots will be formed—and the new plant can be cut off and moved to its own quarters.

Basket begonias are also propagated from seeds and stem cuttings, as described in Chapter 4.

NAMED VARIETIES OF BASKET BEGONIAS

In addition to the varieties described in this chapter, many begonias of other types grow happily and beautifully in hanging baskets. Most angel-wings are effective, if kept low. Many of the rhizomatous and hairy-leaved varieties, and a large selection from other upright and branching begonias, can be planted and grown this way. Check other chapters for these:

Chapter 7—Angel-Wings: 'Helen W. King,' 'Pink Wave.'

Chapter 8—Hairy-Leaved Begonias: 'Alto-Scharff,' 'Houghtoni,' *fernando-costae, scharffiana.*

Chapter 9—Other Upright, Branching Begonias: 'Braemar,' 'Corbeille de Feu,' *cubensis,* 'Digswelliana,' *foliosa,* 'Frutescaria,' 'Mme. Fanny Giron,' 'Richmondensis,' *schmidtiana.*

Chapter 11—Rhizomatous Begonias: *boweri, chimborazo, dayi, hispi-davillosa,* 'Janet Kay,' *liebmanni,* 'Maphil,' *mazae, pustulata, stitched leaf,* 'Virbob.'

Chapter 13—Odd and Rare Begonias: *epipsila, manni.*

FOR BEGINNERS

'Alpha Gere'—1940 hybrid of restrained size and habit, with waxy, wedge-shaped leaves on two-foot trailing stems. Small white flowers hold up their heads at stem tips.

'Limminghei'—Named for garden-owner Count Limminghe. Pointed, shiny green leaves tumble gracefully down along many stems; coral-red flowers in close clusters in late winter. Provide warmth, brightest light, richer soil, more fertilizer than most. Easily propagated by layering. A variation is listed as 'Limmingheiana.'

macrocarpa (Africa)—Name means "large-fruited." Arching stems droop slim-oval leaves of glossy dark green; at the tips, small clusters of palest pink and white flowers.

'Marjorie Daw' (*coccinea* x *glaucophylla*)—Favorite wing-leaved trailer with wavy green foliage, long-lasting clusters of gorgeous pink flowers. Adapts to cool air; dislikes hottest sun. Winter-flowering in sufficient light.

FOR ADVANCED GROWERS

'd 'Artagnon' (*epipsila* x *scharffiana*)—Hairy "Queen of the Basket Begonias" with thick, hoary, curled-up leaves of forest-green, blood-red on the back, like the hat of the fourth musketeer. Dense growth will conceal pot or basket. Needs plenty of light, little water. Translucent green stipules turn brown and wither, but remain.

'Elsie M. Frey' (*baumanni* x 'Limminghei')—Short stems and branches hold metallic-green, red-lined leaves close to the pot; pink flowers in late winter.

'E. O. Orpet' (*mazae* x 'Limmingheiana')—Easier and hardier than either parent. Bronze-green leaves; red beneath; flowers, warm coral in winter.

'Florence Carrell' ('Limminghei' x *incarnata*)—Glossy green, medium-sized leaves, crinkly on the edge; coral flowers.

glabra (Jamaica)—Also listed as *scandens, scandens cordifolia.* Name means "hairless, smooth." At home, this climber sinks roots into the bark of trees as it ascends. On a totem pole, it may do the same. Will also dangle gracefully from a basket. Handsome, high-gloss green leaves in abundance; white flowers.

Basket begonias: TOP row: 'Limminghei,' 'Ivy Ever,' 'Shippy's Garland.'
MIDDLE ROW: 'Florence Carrell,' 'Digswelliana,' 'Elsie M. Frey.' BOTTOM
ROW: 'd'Artagnon,' *scandens, sanguinea.*

'Indra' (*rubro-venia* x *deliciosa*)—Small creeper or climber with well-waxed green leaves, gold-hearted white flowers.

'Ivy Ever' (*martiana* x *glaucophylla scandens*)—Willing brancher and trailer with heart-shaped leaves, glossy dark green, tinged red-purple at the veins; large flowers, showy pink. Guard against mildew.

sanguinea (Brazil)—Name means "blood-red." Thick, leathery, oval leaves, pottery-glazed brown over green on top; red underneath; white flowers. Eagerness to branch from the base makes this a handsome basket plant. A "true species" with thick green leaves was newly introduced or re-introduced in 1959.

'Shippy's Garland' ('Limminghei' x *scandens cordifolia*)—Free-branching trailer with four-inch leaves irregularly notched and crisply crinkled; plenteous bright cherry flowers dangle down for a month or more.

FOR COLLECTORS

convolvulacea (Brazil)—At home, it's a climber. In a basket, it dangles graceful stems with light green oval leaves, white flowers in spring. Keep cool and moist. Propagate from tip cuttings.

'Frutescans' (*fruticosa* seedling)—Low, spreading grower. Leaves similar to, and half the size of, *sanguinea,* with wavy edges. Shy bloomer with small white flowers.

'Lulandi' ('Coralline de Lucerna' x *sutherlandi*)—Angel-wing and tuberous parents created a child which forms a small tuber in the soil, also false bulbils along the stem. Does not go dormant. Should be renewed by stem cuttings at least every other year. Small green leaves; glistening pink flowers. Branches freely.

'Orange Dainty'—Dark green leaves toothed on the edge; delicate orange flowers.

VARIETIES TO WATCH OR WAIT FOR

'Ellen Dee' ('Limminghei' x *dichroa*)—Name derived from initials "L" and "D." Not truly an angel-wing, but somewhat similar. Fresh green foliage and great clusters of orange flowers.

CHAPTER 11

Rhizomatous Begonias

Here is where Nature goes haywire—and begonia fanciers do too. Where could you find so many different types, textures, sizes, and shapes of leaves? Who could believe in such fairy-tale showers of flowers held so light and airy above the foliage? What other kind of plant rewards you for neglect with such stunning and colorful effect, year in and year out?

Rhizomatous begonias will certainly take a lot of punishment. Certain venerable varieties have been known to withstand freeze, blistering heat, and drought; and even when thrown out, have continued to try to grow in the compost or ash heap.

The secret, of course, is the rhizome. Neither a stem nor a root, it is a gnarled, scarred, thick, stemlike root (or rootlike stem) which stores up food and moisture on which the plant can live for quite a while in dry or famine times. In other plant families, rhizomes usually grow in the soil, like bulbs or tubers. But begonia rhizomes stay up on top, sending out stems above and roots below. Some creep, crawl, or snake their way along the top of the soil—horizontally. Of these, some root as they go along; some don't. Other begonia rhizomes grow upward, at a slant, their leaves all facing front. Some branch out; others start new growth only from the base.

Mature rhizomatous begonias bloom once a year, in late winter or early spring, with nodding flower clusters on branching stems held high above the foliage. In flower or not, the plants are outstanding for their spectacular variety of foliage—from the size of a penny to a football, geometrically angular or softly round, streaked and blotched or luxuriantly plain, toothed on the edge or not.

Among the popular leaf shapes is the "star"—with the required five points or more. Star-shaped leaves come in silver, gold-bronze, mahogany, red-brown, and green. They may be nubby, satiny, or brocaded; streaked, blotched, or striped; thick or thin; large or small.

Inappropriately, the popular "pond-lily" leaves belong to a begonia dubbed "beefsteak" for the blood-red color underneath the leaf. This too is available in more ornate frilled, ruffled, crested versions—leading to the nickname "lettuce-leaf begonia."

HOW TO GROW RHIZOMATOUS BEGONIAS

These varieties are usually shallow-rooted, which calls for potting them in a shallow container. The horizontal types flourished in hanging baskets, the rhizomes creeping out over the edge of the basket and down the side. And here's a prize-winning flower-show idea. Train a rhizomatous begonia on a totem pole. Some of the brilliant new hybrids, such as 'Virbob' and 'Maphil,' have been grown this way, presenting a striking display.

Because their root-stem storehouse makes them so self-sufficient, rhizomatous begonias are best grown on the dry side—in soil slightly more light, humusy, porous than the average. They're potted with the rhizome on top of the soil, not in it, the growing tip as far away from the other side of the pot as possible. This gives them more soil surface on which to creep.

Watering is crucial. The rhizome is fleshy, and so subject to rot. Constant hovering with watering pot and fertilizer kills more rhizomatous begonias than all the pests and diseases put together. The larger the leaf, the thicker the rhizome, the less water, is a good working principle. Many varieties do, however, appreciate a daily spray or the creation of some extra humidity.

Winter sunlight is essential, if the plants are to flower in the spring. Artificial light from a reading or table lamp, to extend the short winter day, is of considerable help.

In fall or early winter, many species—and some hybrids—take a semidormant siesta. They may drop a few leaves (don't let it frighten you), or simply stop growing for a while. During this time, withhold fertilizer entirely, water very lightly—until you see signs that new growth is beginning.

HOW TO PROPAGATE RHIZOMATOUS BEGONIAS

All the propagating methods described in Chapter 4 will work for rhizomatous begonias. With seeds, you can increase your collection

'Ricinifolia'   *rubro-venia*   'Leo Shippy'

stitched leaf   'Virbob'

hydrocotylifolia   'Erythrophylla Helix'

                                        strigillosa

carolineaefolia   'Silver Star'   'Fuscomaculata'

RHIZOMATOUS BEGONIAS

of otherwise hard-to-find species and some well-established hybrids. With rhizome cuttings, you can have strong, sturdy new plants in record time. Some varieties even produce plantlets spontaneously on the rhizome, near soil level, which can be taken off and potted.

Leaf cuttings are a slower but popular method of producing new plants. Two-inch stems are inserted at an angle in the rooting medium in a prop box—hardier varieties, occasionally, in a glass of water. New plants usually appear at the stem end, African-violet style; only occasionally at the point where leaf and stem meet, rex-begonia style. But you may need to cultivate patience. These new plants frequently do not acquire the parent's desirable variations in leaf shape, frilled edge, variegated color, until they are nearly or fully mature.

NAMED VARIETIES OF RHIZOMATOUS BEGONIAS

These are classified according to ease of culture and availability, as items for beginners, advanced growers, and collectors; also, new items to watch for in the future. Recently, new species have been brought back from Brazil which promise to make this fascinating group of begonias more colorful and intriguing than ever.

FOR BEGINNERS

'Beatrice Haddrell' (*boweri* x *sunderbruchi*)—Small, sharply pointed star leaf basically rich black; light green sunburst effect at stem end radiates out in irregular streaks along veins. Large and plentiful pink flowers tower above in spring.

'Bessie Buxton'—Named for the New England begonia authority. An upright-growing form of the old favorite "beefsteak" or "pond-lily" begonia, 'Erythrophylla,' with thinner but otherwise similar leaves, pink flowers. Grows best on the dry side.

boweri hybrids—A group partially named for the female parent, and illustrating the power of the dominant characteristics. All are dwarf or miniature; all have reflections of the eyelash edging; all bear pink flowers. 'Bow-Arriola (*boweri* x *C42*), named for the comic-strip artist, has star leaves, green with purple markings along the veins and edge. 'Bow-Chancee' has yellow-green leaves blanket-stitched with chocolate. 'Bow-Joe' (*boweri* x 'Joe Hay-

den') has small star leaves, dark-complexioned, like the father.
'Bow-Nigra' (*boweri* x *heracleifolia nigricans*) has star-shaped
bronzy leaves with much lighter veins.

'Brocade' ('Silver Star' seedling)—Star-leaved queen with leaves of
iridescent purple-silver highlighted by an uneven, bumpy textile
texture. Tends to grow upright. Flowers white.

'Bunchi'—'Lettuce-leaved" sport of 'Erythrophylla,' with frilled
edges revealing gay red-leathery lining on back of leaf. An old
stand-by, more loved as the years go by. Pink flowers. Leaf cuttings may produce plain leaves which will frill in time.

charlotta (India)—Probably a variety of *acetosa* with shorter stems;
round, thick, slightly cupped leaves, drab green above, royal-purple plush beneath.

'Erythrophylla' (*hydrocotylifolia* x *manicata*)—Name means "red
leaf." Also called 'Feasti'—or "pond-lily" or "beefsteak" begonia.
This venerable hybrid always puts on a terrific show—spectacular
in its spring bloom. Round leaves are tough but polished to a
high green gloss, violent red underneath. Withstands most problems and pests with aplomb.

'Erythrophylla Helix'—Spiraled sport. Popularly called the "cork-
screw" begonia. Round leaves curl, and large lobes overlap at the
stem. For a frillier version of the same plant, see 'Bunchi.'

heracleifolia (Mexico)—Name means "like the cow parsnip." Pink-
flowered, robust star-leaf, available in several varieties: plain
green leaf; *nigricans* with white flowers, leaves so dark green
they're nearly black; *pyramidalis,* medium green; *sunderbruchi,*
variegated green and black; and *venus.*

'Joe Hayden' ('Reichenheimi' x *mazae*)—Large, dark-sheened star
leaves with bright cream spot at stem; red lining beneath gives
reversible effect; dark color in little sun gives rise to nickname
"black begonia." Vigorous rhizome creeps, divides, creates shapely
plant. Red flower buds open white. A smaller version is offered
as 'Joe Hayden, Jr.'

manicata (Mexico)—Name means "cuffed," or "long-sleeved"—
refers to the collar of hairs around the stem where it joins the
leaf. Upright type with sturdy rhizome; nearly round, glossy green
leaf; collar of stiff red bristles at the top of stem, under leaf.
Plantlets pop up on rhizome near soil, can be carefully lifted
and potted.

'Maphil' or 'Cleopatra' (*boweri* seedling)—Once-in-a-lifetime treasure with every dreamy virtue: well-mannered growing habits—restrained size in pot or basket, small call for pampering; eye-stopping foliage—sprightly satin stars with sharply marked veins, artistically spattered between with gold or chartreuse and chocolate-brown; fairy-tale sprays of baby pink flowers; also readily available.

'Ricinifolia' (*heracleifolia* x *peponifolia*)—Name refers to *ricinus,* the castor-bean plant, which has similar leaves. Illustrious old-time parlor specimen speeds from rooted rhizome cutting to big and blooming the first year. Foot-long green star leaves on tall, strong stems; pink flowers. Healthy and hardy. 'Fischer's Ricinifolia' is a slightly smaller, more compact variation.

'Ricky Minter' (*cristata* x *mazae*)—Named for a little boy. Crisp, lusty, lobed leaves lavishly frilled and crested on the edge. Color light bronze-green in some sun, to dark green near black in shade. Flowers pink. Easy to grow—on the dry side; and propagate—leaf-stem or rhizome cuttings. A good bet for a flower-show prize.

'Silver Star' (*carolineaefolia* x *liebmanni*)—An outstanding hybrid with medium-sized star leaves iridescent rosy-silver; margins somewhat waved. Pink tint on white flowers.

sunderbruchi (variety of *heracleifolia*)—Old-fashioned favorite "star" or "finger-leaf begonia." Seven- or nine-fingered leaves are large, bronze-green, strikingly marked with light green veins and splotches, mottled red and green beneath. Each finger is pointed, and scalloped on the edge. Stems ringed with collar of red hairs at joining with leaf. Two-petaled pink flowers.

FOR ADVANCED GROWERS

acetosa (Brazil)—Name means "acid, sour." Neat, round, hairy leaves top short stilt stems from rhizome below. On top, the effect of fuzz is subdued green; underneath, ruby-red. Proportionate sprays of white flowers in spring.

boweri (Mexico)—Named for begonia-grower Bower. "Eyelash begonia," with delicate green leaves stitched with black on the edge—regular eyelash bristles. Sprays of shell-pink flowers. May be temperamental on a window sill; demands protection, humidity,

ODD AND RARE BEGONIAS

TOP ROW: *venosa, aridicaulis, kenworthyi.* MIDDLE ROW: *acida, hemsleyana.*
BOTTOM ROW: *luxurians, manni, deliciosa.*

Rhizomatous begonias: TOP ROW: 'Maphil,' *manicata aureo-maculata.*
MIDDLE ROW: *iron cross, boweri, imperialis.* BOTTOM ROW: 'Brocade,'
'Ricky Minter.'

and light humusy soil. Creeps on top of soil in shallow pot, likes baskets. Good subject for terrariums—grows to specimen stature in sphagnum moss.

boweri major (Mexico)—Larger-leaved variety of the species; leaves plainer; similar habit and tastes.

'Congo'—Upright grower with small, very dark green leaves, lighter-tinted veins running from stem end to each sharp point. Pink flowers.

'Crestabruchi' (*manicata crispa* x *sunderbruchi*)—Show-off with glossy yellow-green leaves heavily curled and twisted on the edge, blotched with cream. Flowers pink. Rests after late-winter flowering; repot at new growth in June. Leaf-steam and rhizome cuttings root fairly easily; leaf wedges more slowly.

dayi (Mexico)—Named for importer Day. Large, thick, shiny leaves more yellow than green, the veins heavily penciled with dark mahogany on top, dark red underneath. Sometimes called *nigrovenia*, or "black-veined." Flowers ivory. Likes to grow warm and dryish.

'Ella Keyes' ('Erythrophylla' x 'Mrs. Townsend')—Upright type, inheriting large, round leaves and pink flowers from its mother.

'Fuscomaculata' (*heracleifolia* x *strigillosa*)—Name means "brown-spotted." Sometimes listed as 'Rubellina.' Individualist with gray-green, star-shaped leaves lightly chocolate-splotched, drooping on long, lax stems. Shy bloomer; rests in winter.

'Heracleicotyle' or 'Mrs. Townsend.' (*heracleifolia* x *hydrocotylifolia*) Large, seven-pointed-star leaves of fresh, clean green; beautiful deep pink flowers.

hispidavillosa (Mexico)—Name means "semistiff-hairy." Round, hairy leaves divided into pie wedges by sunken veins which meet and make a bright eye at the stem end. Flowers, white. Happiest in a moss-lined wire basket.

hydrocotylifolia (Mexico)—Name means "leaves like the water penny-wort." Called the "miniature pond-lily begonia." Terrarium-type creeper with round leaves the size of an English penny, glossy and vein-shadowed. Midwinter flowers, pink on six-inch stems. Plant in your most shallow container or basket.

'Illustrata' ('Speculata' x *imperialis*)—Name means "brilliant, lustrous." Variously described as "round-" or "grape-leaved," the plant appears in a 1953 photograph as having plenteous dainty leaves, rounded to a sharp point, shimmering with a coat of fine white hairs; pinkish midwinter flowers.

imperialis (Mexico)—Name means "imperial," "royal." Tenderly pointed round leaf upholstered in finely nubbed olive-brown plush, emerald-green at the veins. The variety *smaragdina* (meaning "emerald") is smoother, solid brilliant green. Seedlings may range in markings and texture between the two. Keep warm and humid. Leaf cuttings do best if kept on the dry side.

iron cross (Malaya)—Now, correctly, *masoniana,* for English discoverer Mason. Sensational plant with gold-green leaves thickly nubby, and centered with a mahogany replica of the German iron cross—which may fade in too-bright sun. Requires careful watering—roots rot when too wet; leaf edges crisp when too dry. Slow but fairly sure from seeds.

'Legacy' ('Silver Star' seedling)—Glossy, bronze-green star leaves with tapering center point, red-lined beneath; white flowers. Upright grower with commendable inclination to branch.

'Leo C. Shippy' ('Ricinifolia' seedling)—Seven-pointed star leaf, each point further cut and crinkled; striking bright green accented with red veins. Red-hairy underside bewhiskers the leaf edges, also gives a glowing effect in strong light. Large clusters of pink flowers.

liebmanni (Mexico)—Named for collector Liebmann. Green, modified star leaves gently dusted with silver splashes; light purple underneath. Rhizome is slender, roots readily as its creeps, hangs over the edge of the pot with the appearance of a stem. Specially suitable for wire baskets, totem pole, or moss wall.

manicata varieties—All with characteristic collar of hairs around stem. Variety *crispa,* or *cristata,* has all-green leaves with crested edge; *aureo-maculata* has smooth green leaves blotched with cream and yellow; *aureo-maculata crispa* has yellow-blotched leaves with crested edge; may be listed as *aureo-cristata.*

mazae (Mexico)—Named for owner of the ranch where it was found. Round leaves with tiny pointed tail, bronze-green marked red-brown along the light veins which meet in a white eye; deep red underneath. Small, light pink, red-spotted flowers. Grow warm, protected, fairly dry, with perfect drainage. *Stitched leaf* is probably a variety of this species.

nelumbifolia (Mexico)—Named for the nelumbo water lily. Leaves peltate (stem attached near center, not on edge), lotus-leaf fashion. Foot-long leaves, green, round at top, pointed at the end, with hairs beneath. Flowers, small, white to palest pink. An even more striking 'Red-Veined Nelumbifolia,' a seedling, is sometimes available.

'Pearli'—Creeping rhizome hidden by hordes of pebbled and bristly jade-green leaves overlaid with pearly pink. Sometimes classified as "grape-leaf." Shuns sunlight.

'Reichenheimi' (*heracleifolia* x 'Fuscomaculata')—Rhizome snakes and curls along the soil. Leaves green with red-bronze veins, typically star-shaped. Pink flowers. Often drops some leaves just before blooming. Grows on the dry side.

rotundifolia (Haiti)—Name means "round-leaved." Pygmy creeper stays terrarium-size for years. Penny-shaped leaves, yellowish green; flowers, pink.

'Sir Percy' ('Silver Star' x 'Speculata')—Trouble-free, full-leaved plant looks much like a rex but is easier to care for. Pointed silver-plated leaves show a penciled edge of dark green.

'Skeezar' (*dayi* x *liebmanni*)—Whimsically christened creation with small, modified star leaves marbled green and silvery white. 'Green Skeezar' has plain green leaves faced with red. Some new variations are also in the offing.

'Spaulding' (*boweri* x *hydrocotylifolia*)—Named for former American Begonia Society President. Bushy dwarf with coin-round leaves shaded velvety grass-green to darkest green, oxblood underneath, bewhiskered on the edge. Pink flowers.

stitched leaf—A variety of *mazae*. Leaves satiny spinach-green, blanket-stitched with black along the edge. Looks straggly when left to grow at will; but when rhizome is pinned to soil at intervals, eyes root and throw out branches—a fuller, more shapely appearance. Lovely in baskets.

strigillosa, or *daedalea*—Name means "sharp-haired." Chocolate-spotted, roundish green leaves on long stems; curry-comb hairs on the edge. Flowers, pink.

'Suncana' (*sunderbruchi* x *incana*)—Egg-shaped, slightly pointed leaves felted with brown fuzz; white flowers.

'Tamo' (*incana* x *mazae*)—Erect and freely branching from the base. Three-inch pointed green leaves, dark green above, fuzzy red below; blanket-stitched on the edge. Flowers, white.

'Verschaffelti' (*manicata* x *carolineaefolia*)—Handsome, stately giant with large, ascending rhizome notched like a gun. Thick, wavy, round green leaves slightly cut to six points; clear pink flowers.

'Zee Bowman' (*boweri* seedling)—Silvery, star-leaved miniature with pleasing compact shape, pink flowers.

FOR COLLECTORS

barbana (Costa Rica)—Leaves of medium size, medium green, traced with reddish veins; stems and underleaf hairy.

'Bright Eyes' (*C42* x 'John R.')—Fragrant-flowered star begonia with silky, firm, black-green leaves, outstanding for the bright green eye at the stem end; dark red below. Loose panicles of light pink flowers with rosy hearts.

'Carol Star' (*carolineaefolia* x *sunderbruchi*)—Upright type with broad, glossy green leaves cut almost to the stem end, saw-toothed on the edge. Strong and spectacular.

carolineaefolia (Mexico)—Name means "leaves like the Carolina, or *Pachira*, tree." Trunklike rhizome to three inches in diameter grows upright; seldom branches; will send out new shoots when tip is cut off. Large leaves resembling the horse chestnut; seven to nine neatly fluted green leaflets attached to the stem end. Spires of rosy flowers. Majestic.

chimborazo (Guatemala)—Named for Ecuadorian mountain. Shiny, cupped, nasturtium-like leaves with yellow veins; stems often lax. Pink flowers open to white. A creeper.

circumlobata (China)—Name means "lobed all around." Leaves like a Chinese umbrella, but cut deeply to the stem end. Fairly fast grower, must not be pot-bound. Watch watering carefully—grow drier than most.

conchaefolia (Costa Rica)—Name means "shell-shaped leaves." Thickish, juicy green leaves above creeping rhizome cup up slightly. Small enough for a large terrarium. Winter-blooming. Grows on trees in Costa Rica.

'Dark Sheen'—Semidwarf *boweri* hybrid with leaves angled and dark on the edge.

decora (Brazil)—Name means "elegant." Coveted species with sweet-scented white flowers; plushy brown-green leaves sharply etched with light veins.

'Eloise' (*imperialis* x *scharffiana*)—Petite charmer with small, dark green leaves, pale pink flowers.

francisi (Mexico)—Nicknamed "nasturtium-leaved." Slim rhizome twists and turns along the soil, rooting as it goes along. Leaves, glossy and cupped; stems, red.

fusca (Mexico)—Name means "dusky, tawny, grayish-brown." Tremendous soft green leaves scalloped on the edge, on long stems, from large rhizome. Striking white eye where veins converge on stem. Magnificent specimen at the Montreal Botanical Gardens.

handelli (China)—Named for composer Handel. Semi-upright type with large, fuzzy leaves—distinguished by the spicy fragrance of its white flowers.

'Helen Krauss' (*dayi* x *mazae*)—Named for begonia authority. Larger, stronger, *mazae*-like leaves nearly needly-pointed at the tip; satiny spinach-green with bitter-chocolate veins. On tall, red stems, dark red flowers lined inside with pale pink.

hepatica maculata (Mexico)—Name means "spotted liver leaf." Low, sprawly plant with brown markings on round, sand-yellow leaves.

'Illsley' (*boweri* x *mazae*)—Miniature with dark green eyelashed leaves, pink flowers.

'Immense' ('Ricinifolia' seedling)—Immense star leaves, softer and more lustrous than 'Ricinifolia'; ascending rhizome; pink flowers.

'Inglewood' (*sunderbruchi* x *manicata*)—Sturdy grower with crisply ruffled, red-bronze, fingered leaves, glowing pink flowers.

'Kumwha' (*kenworthyi* x 'Reichenheimi')—Large-leaved, free-blooming star type—a fairly new hybrid not yet in wide distribution.

laciniata bowringiana (India)—Name means "cut into narrow lobes." Rex-looking leaf with angular points, sharply marked zones in three shades of green; large pink flowers.

'Lettonica' (*heracleifolia* x *nelumbifolia*)—Massive-looking plant with thick, upright rhizome and shallow-cut, brown-hairy leaves; pink flowers.

'Liebestar' (*liebmanni* x 'Silver Star')—From curling rhizome, eight-inch stems hold up silvery-green star leaves with crinkly edges, red-flushed beneath, unusually spiraled at the stem end. Pink flowers.

'Madame Queen' (*manicata aureo-maculata crispa* x 'Leslie Lynn')—

Newly released hybrid with portly mahogany-red leaves femininely frilled on the edge.

'Marian' ('Ricinifolia' seedling)—Somewhat less gigantic, but more glamorous than the parent plant; more colorful leaves, bronzy with red beneath.

'Michael L. Barnes' ('Fuscomaculata' seedling)—Medium-green heart-shaped leaves with tapering points, chocolate spots. One of the few rhizomatous types blooming (pink) in summer.

'Mrs. Mary Peace' ('Ricinifolia' x *carolineaefolia*)—Named for California grower. Leaves more like the palm than a star, neatly veined with bright green. Creeping rhizome. Likes warmth, protection.

'Muriel Day' (*imperialis* x *liebmanni*)—Medium-green, pimpled leaves; heavily stroked silver along the veins; contrasting red beneath. Creamy white flowers.

'Niagara'—Large plant with proportionate heart-shaped olive leaves; red-veined beneath. Large white flower heads fragrant and long-lasting.

'Page 13' (Mexico)—Named for page 13, *The Journal of the New York Botanical Garden,* where it was first described. Probably a hybrid, with a creeping rhizome sending up long stems topped by near-round, brown-flecked green leaves. Pink flowers.

pinetorum (Mexico)—Heavy-textured leaves, brown flannel underneath, fuzzy white over lemon-green on top; scalloped edge trimmed with a brown pencil line. Flowers pink.

popenoei (Honduras)—Named for discoverer Popenoe. Giant with bright green leaves, white flowers. Grows happily in wet tropical forests; demands winter rest. Keep warm and dryish until new growth shows.

pustulata (Mexico)—Name means "blistered." Species similar to *imperialis,* with heavier bumps, fewer hairs. Flowers, rose-pink. The dark, plain-leaved version not often seen. *Pustulata argentea* ("Silver pustulata") has irregular silver streaks; requires warmth and humidity; likes moss-lined wire basket.

rubro-venia (India)—Name means "red-veined." Small rhizome hides under the thick shelter of tapering, lance-shaped leaves. There are four variations—light-green-leaved; dark green; silvery leaves lined with red; and cream-splotched or spotted. Easy to grow from seed or stem cuttings.

schulziana (Haiti)—Sometimes labeled *kraussiana*. Named for grower Schulz. Intriguing individualist that tends to its own propagation. After flowering time in late fall, the miniature white-fuzzed leaves fall off; plant sleeps without disturbance all winter. By spring, the rhizome has broken up into little rooted pieces, each for its own new pot and new growth. Likes warmth, shallow pot.

'Sementacea' (Brazil)—May be a natural hybrid. Grown side by side in the Montreal Botanical Gardens, a near twin of new *vellozoana,* and equally lush and covetable. Veins strikingly etched on iridescent silk-satin green leaf.

sparsipila (Central America)—Unbranched, upright type, completely covered with a coat of fine felt. Pink flowers.

squamosa (Costa Rica)—Name means "scaly." Creeping dwarf with glossy green, red-rimmed leaves on longish, limp stems; pink flowers. The scales are on the stems.

tenuifolia (Java)—Name means "thin-leaved." Upright and short-branched. Many-pointed, tapering leaves deep green above, lighter below, with rosy veins. Large, abundant, delicate pink flowers.

'Verde Grande' (*manicata* x 'Dark Sheen')—Name means "green giant." Exceptionally fine new star leaf of smoothest green satin, trimmed with blue-black braided markings on the edge; pale eye and radiating veins. Strong, vigorous, and adaptable.

'Virbob' (*boweri* seedling)—Prize-winning dwarf with perky autumn-red star leaves divided by chartreuse veins running to the tips of the small, sharp points; bright red beneath. Outstanding for the way the short stems cup the leaves close to the pot, completely covering it. Flowers, pink. A basket beauty.

'Zaida' (*mazae* x *epipsila*)—Compact dwarf with bronze-veined, dark green, roundish leaves.

VARIETIES TO WATCH OR WAIT FOR

'Alice-Mac' and 'Mac-Alice' (*imperialis* x *macdougalli*)—Twin seedlings with pimpled, lobed leaves, silvery sheen over aqua-green.

'Buckskin Baby'—Star-leaved midget with elfin charm. New.

'Carol Imp' (*carolineaefolia* x *sunderbruchi* or *imperialis*)—'Speculata'-like, grape-shaped leaves, but smaller and irregularly lobed, light green and puckered with white-haired bumps. Small white flowers.

'Cathy Lou'—Abundance of small star leaves, bronze-splotched green edged with white eyelashes. Flowers, pink.

'Cool Waters'—Satiny, dark green star leaves, lighter along the stems.

'Edith M.' (*boweri* x 'Reichenheimi').

'Elsa Fort' (*imperialis* x *mazae*)—Red-backed, dark green leaf, slightly hairy; small clusters of red-dotted pink flowers.

'Emerald Jewel'—See 'Silver Jewel.'

'Fleecealba' (*sunderbruchi* x *woolly bear*)—Upright grower with white-felted thick green leaves, many white flowers.

'Fred Brown' (*pinetorum* x *mazae*).

'Freddie' (*manicata aureo-maculata* x *barkeri*)—Grows fast and furiously. Magnificent specimen with giant, bronze-green, red-backed leaves and showers of pink flowers.

'Glendale' (*sunderbruchi* seedling)—Star-leaved medal winner grows full and compact. Leaves, bright green with lighter veins, brownish between; maroon and green beneath.

'Gypsy Marie' (*ecuadorensis* x *mazae*).

'Inzae' (*involucrata* x *mazae*)—Pointed, edge-stitched leaf of medium size and color.

'Jane' (*imperialis* x *mazae*).

'Janet Kay' (*imperialis* x *francisi*).

'Jocko' ('Leslie Lynn' seedling)—Long-stemmed, dark red, modified-star leaf.

'John R.' (*dayi* x *macdougalli*).

'Kongo' (*kenworthyi* x *mazae*).

'Lake' group (*dayi* x *imperialis maculata*)—Newly registered hybrids with thin, heart-shaped leaves; white flowers in summer. 'Blue Lake' leaves are green; 'Crystal Lake,' green with silver between veins; 'Oneda Lake,' green faced with oxblood; 'Ada Lake,' green with brown veins, raised silver areas.

'Leslie Lynn' ('Lexington' x *dayi*)—Strong, sturdy new hybrid with satiny star-shaped leaves.

macdougalli (Mexico)—Enormous-leaved giant like a stately, waving palm. Perfect specimen may be seen growing in four-foot urn at Montreal Botanical Gardens.

'Otto Alfred' (*strigillosa* x *burkei*)—Large, flat, pointed green leaves generously flecked with brown.

'Pebble Lane' ('Speculata' x 'Sir Percy')—Rex-like, pebbly leaves, marbelized brown-green, topped by large silver areas different in size and shape on each leaf; edge, dark green. Grows quickly to full, bushy shape.

'Poplar' (*acida* x 'Pearli').

'Red Bluff' ('Dark Sheen' x *manicata*).

'Rosanna'—Lustrous, large green star leaf on full, well-shaped plant.

rupicola—Name means "rock-dweller." Yellow-spattered, heart-shaped green leaves; pink flowers.

'Sacramento Star' (*mazae* x *macdougalli*).

'Silver Jewel' (*imperialis* x *pustulata*)—This and 'Emerald Jewel,' both of the same cross, have all of *imperialis's* glamour but less of its touchy temperament. 'Silver Jewel' has silver between green veins; conversely, 'Emerald Jewel' has green areas between silver-overlaid veins.

'Skeezar' group—A number of newly registered hybrids (*dayi* x *liebmanni*) with varying modified star leaves. 'Skeezar Mirror Lake' has green leaves overlaid with silver; 'Skeezar Frosty Lake' has green leaves, unevenly silver along the veins, reddish on back; 'Skeezar Brown Lake' has green leaves above, oxblood below; surfaces are fine-hairy.

'Venice' (*acetosa* x *venosa*)—Medium-sized hairy leaves, heavy, reversible light green and pinkish. Compact grower.

xanthina (India)—Name means "yellow." Densely bushy plant with yellow-veined green leaves, large orange-yellow flowers.

CHAPTER 12

Rex Begonias

"In variety of texture, color, and pattern the rex begonias exceed all the fantasies that have ever been woven in brocade." Believe it or not, this is an understatement. Since that sentence was written by one of the begonia family's most talented admirers, in 1951, hybridists have created foliage with fabulously brilliant and textured effects beyond anyone's wildest dreams.

Think of the jewel colors—amethyst, ruby, aquamarine, garnet, topaz, emerald, opal, and pearl. The rexes have them all. Picture the precious metals—gold, silver, platinum, antique bronze. Rex foliage gleams like them. Run the gamut of fabric textures, modern or not —silk, satin, velvet, taffeta, brocade; nubby tweeds and soft, fuzzy woolens; novelty cottons; the miracle fabrics. Singly or in combination, you'll find all colors, textures, and finishes in the glorious group of rex begonias. The popular names—"painted," "pallet," "caladium," and "king's begonia"—are well earned and deserved.

Flower-arrangement devotees will offer their right arms for rex leaves to complete a composition. A gemlike rex enthroned in a corner of a greenhouse stops visitors in their tracks. Of all passionate plant hobbyists, those who have become enthralled with rex begonias have the most insatiable thirst for more brilliant varieties, and more space to grow them in.

All this came about by accident. The original *Begonia rex* was discovered growing in the pot of an orchid imported into England in 1856. Every begonia bearing the rex name is one of its descendants. Other rarely lovely begonias have contributed royal blood to the strain, but only to improve it—never to replace it.

Of all hybrid begonias, rexes have the most complicated ancestry. Every one of today's rexes is the result of crossing one rex with another, or a rex with another type of begonia species or hybrid. And any rex used in making the cross was created in the same way. After its sensational discovery, the original species was crossed and recrossed with other exotics (*xanthina, griffithi, laciniata,* to name a few) and, having blessed the world with some of its most gorgeous foliage plants, *B. rex* left the stage to its offspring and retired to obscurity.

This is why those who are serious about neat and orderly nomenclature are frustrated when they run afoul of the rexes. Two plants so nearly identical in leaf color, pattern, and texture that close comparison can't tell them apart can spring up at the same time—but from two different seed pods sown by growers unaware of each other's existence. Each grower names his new pride and joy according to his fancy; and soon the market is enriched with near twins bearing entirely different names. Rex nomenclature is sometimes so confused that both suppliers and buyers ignore names completely. You simply make your choice according to the colors or patterns that please you.

Rex begonias are all more or less rhizomatous in nature, the majority with the characteristic scrubby, scarred rhizome twisting its way across the top of the soil. All rexes produce water-lily-like, porcelain-pure flowers in shades of pink and white, usually hidden under—and overshadowed by—the magnificent foliage.

Some general types of rex leaf formation and coloring can be singled out. The lovely varieties with thin, soft, velvety leaves are generally more difficult to grow than those with tougher, rougher texture. The increasing new group of dwarfs and miniatures is, sadly, still on the finicky side, but breeders should soon bring them up to snuff. Some beautiful new German rexes have been bred specifically for vigor and hardiness.

Rex fanciers speak of the "spirals"—leaves with one exaggerated lobe which overlaps and curls around like a winding staircase. "Diadema type" refers to a group of rexes to which one parent, *B. diadema,* bequeathed sharp geometric patterns and angles, and a sharp-tapered point.

HOW TO GROW REX BEGONIAS

Let's face it—these are not the easiest of all begonias to grow. But when did rich rewards ever come without expending some effort?

First, two tips for beginners. Select, to start with, varieties which are recommended for their vigor (there are a goodly number) and, particularly, varieties with leaves which seem crisp and hard rather than limp and soft. And, if you can, buy your first rex begonias in

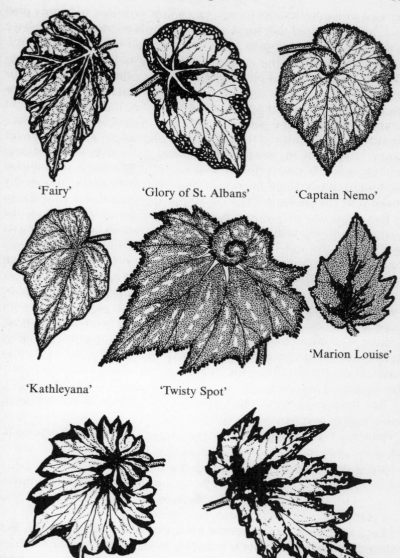

'Fairy'   'Glory of St. Albans'   'Captain Nemo'

'Kathleyana'   'Twisty Spot'   'Marion Louise'

'Winter Queen'   'Bertha McGregor'

REX BEGONIAS

the spring, at the beginning of their good growing season, so they can become established and on their way toward healthy maturity before the difficult winter months roll around.

Which brings us to the subject of dormancy. In late fall and winter, some rexes simply stop growing for a while; others may look sickly for a few weeks or a month and then perk up; and others drop every single precious leaf and go into a deep sleep until early spring.

Some varieties of rex are more likely to go completely dormant than others; some come out of it more quickly and surely; and some growing conditions—cool, dry air, for example—seem to favor dormancy.

The important fact is this. If your beautiful rex drops all its leaves in the fall, don't be disheartened and discard it. Gently pinch the rhizome. If it feels firm and lively, let the plant rest. Set it aside where it can keep warm, protected, and slightly moist. Most likely, in earliest spring, you will see tender new shoots which promise new and even more lovely life.

At any time of year, keep your rexes out of drafts or chill wind, the temperature slightly higher than average (70° or more), and the air as humid as possible. Crisp, dry leaf edges are the product of dry air.

Pot rexes in a soil mixture that is extra light and humusy, with perfect drainage in the pot. Pot lightly—don't pack—in shallow, porous clay pots. The roots are surface growers and feeders. And to keep dwarfs in dwarf size, miniatures in miniature proportions, use pots as small as possible without choking the plants.

Rex begonias grow moist, but never soggy-wet. On the other hand, if they inadvertently dry out and wilt, they will revive quickly when the pot is soaked in water to its rim.

The rexes dislike sun, except the mildest. Leaf coloring is more glowing and brilliant in strong but sunless light.

Since the rexes are grown primarily for their fine foliage, many growers remove buds to prevent flowering, and to let the plant throw its strength into more glorious leaves—also, some say, to conserve the plant's strength when winter is approaching.

In greenhouses, rex begonias are frequently grown beneath the bench. This may be simply for shading from the hot summer sun, or a year-round practice. Many growers plant them, out of their pots, with their roots in three or more inches of soil in a large flat or bench tray. Rexes seem to luxuriate this way, as you might with your feet in comfortable old shoes.

Rex begonias: TOP ROW: 'Helen Teupel,' 'Merry Christmas.' MIDDLE
ROW: 'It,' 'Dewdrop,' 'Baby Rainbow.' BOTTOM ROW: 'Peacock,' 'Curly
Silver Sweet,' 'Black Knight.'

Without doubt, there are few more satisfactory plants for growing under artificial light. Temperature and humidity can be easily controlled. A good fluorescent setup seems to produce just the right kind of light for unblemished leaves of unsurpassed brilliance.

HOW TO PROPAGATE REX BEGONIAS

Prolific is the word for these plants. They reproduce themselves easily, and in a hurry. Some are so eager, in fact, they will voluntarily send up new, viviparous plantlets on leaves attached to the parent plant. The rexes can be propagated in almost every known manner, including division and layering of the rhizome.

Seeds

Because they are such complicated hybrids, rex begonias will not come true from seed. In fact, one seed pod seldom produces two plants alike. The lure is the possibility of producing an outstanding new variety, or increasing a colorful collection of unnamed plants.

Rex seeds are touchy about warmth—bottom heat is helpful—and require three weeks, sometimes more, to germinate. Sow the seed specially thin, so the tender plantlets can grow undisturbed as long as possible before transplanting. In other words, don't transplant until the seedlings have produced their second set of true leaves.

Don't look for striking characteristics in rex seedlings until at least the fourth leaf has unfolded and is fairly mature. And don't expect even this to be permanent. Rex seedlings can change color, texture, size, and habit at any time during the first three years of their young life. Pay particularly careful attention to any slow-growing "runts." They sometimes turn out to be the prized new varieties you've been looking for.

Rhizome Cuttings

This fast and sure propagating method, described in Chapter 4, is generally bypassed because it mutilates a prize plant. But rhizome cuttings can be lifesavers when a rex is starting to rot, or to die from some other cause. The smallest section of healthy rhizome, with the unhealthy tissue trimmed away, can be placed half in and half out of the medium in a propagating box, and will often miraculously root, live, and grow.

Rex begonia leaf cuttings: box holds whole leaves and sections inserted with stem in water, in propagating medium, or pinned flat on medium. 'Silver Sweet,' in back row right, has been potted and the old leaf trimmed away. In front, whole leaf with new plant; leaf wedge and plant; rooted stem cutting of upright 'Lavender Glow,' which will also produce new plants from leaves.

Leaf Cuttings

Here is where rex begonias go delightfully mad. With any one of several different methods, one leaf will produce from one to a dozen new plantlets, and in a manner that's unique in the plant world. Actually, California growers, who propagate monstrous numbers of rexes, simply chop the leaves into pieces of odd sizes, let them fall on a moist propagating medium where the air is warm and humid, and every piece soon sends up tiny leaflets. One of these propagating beds, after the plantlets are started, looks like a thick, Technicolor forest.

Leaf-stem cuttings are the easiest and surest method for the beginner. Cut the leaf with about two inches of stem attached. Insert the stem end in a glass of water—or in a medium like sand, peat, vermiculite, or a mixture—in some humidifying device like a prop box. In as little as three weeks, inch-long roots will have grown out from the stem; and (here is where rexes are madly different) at the point where stem joins leaf, there will appear a tuft or rosette of bushy new growth. Pot the cutting with this rosette resting on the soil, keep it warm, protected, and humid—and watch the rosette grow into a brand-new bushy plant. Trim off the parent leaf when the newcomer has four or more good-sized leaves.

Rex leaves can also be cut into from three to five pie-slice pieces, each with a portion of a main vein running through the center to the point of the slice. Insert these, at an angle and with the wide side up, a half-inch or so deep in a rooting medium. Each leaf section will root and produce a new plant in record time.

In the picturesque, old-time method (which may sometimes disappoint the inexperienced), the main veins of a whole leaf are slit part way through, on the back of the leaf. The very short stem end is put in the rooting medium, and the leaf is laid flat on the medium and pinned down with hairpins, weighted with small stones, or held down by strips of paper or tape. New plants which appear at points where the veins were slit can be carefully removed and potted up, and the leaf replaced to give birth to another batch of babies.

NAMED VARIETIES OF REX BEGONIAS

Unnamed rex begonias are often offered for sale, in groups according to leaf colors and shapes—silver-leaved varieties, brilliant-colored leaves, spirals, dwarfs, and the like. The named varieties offered by specialists can be fairly clearly classified, according to ease of culture and availability, as items of interest to beginners, advanced growers, and collectors. Also, a number of exciting new rexes have been publicized which are well worth waiting and hunting for.

FOR BEGINNERS

'A. D. Davis'—Moderate-sized leaves in changeable silver-gray; margin trimmed with band of complementary brown.

'Can-Can'—Taffeta-crisp leaves with indented veins, deeply dipped and pointed along the edge, entirely metallic-iridescent fuchsia on silver.

'Crimson Glow'—Good-sized lavender-pink leaves with silvery overtones.

'Fairy'—Pointed leaf, basically green, heavily overlaid with silver. Tints pink in good light. Medium size.

'Helen Teupel'—Geometrically angled and patterned leaf in sharply contrasting silver and maroon zones.

'King Edward IV'—Large, red-purple leaves, bumpy, with lighter rose spots.

'Lavender Glow'—Soft leaf, bright orchid blending into dark purple border and center. Upright, branching growth. Stem cuttings root speedily.

'Merry Christmas,' or 'Ruhrtal'—Gay holiday stripes of red, green, silver on firm-textured, pointed leaf with angular edge.

'Peter Pan'—Dark green leaves banded with silver; easy to grow.

'Robin'—Also listed as 'Thrush.' Silver-salted maroon maple leaf; generous bright pink flowers. Upright and branching. One of those that often sends up plantlets at the stem end on a growing leaf.

'Rose Marie'—Crisp, hardy leaves massed on dwarf plant—changeable, taffeta-like pink, lavender, silver.

'Salamander'—Sturdy little plant with pointed leaves standing out like rabbits' ears—basic color silver, divided at even the finest veins by dark green.

'Silver Dawn'—Miniature, with many small, pointed, textured blackgreen leaves splashed with silver.

'Silver Sweet'—A beginner's delight, responds willingly to minimum care. Upright and branching, with green-veined metallic-silver leaves. Propagates readily from leaves or stem cuttings, makes a big, bushy plant in a hurry. More delicate 'Curly Silver Sweet' is so deeply ruffled you can hardly see the stems.

'Speculata'—Blistered "grape-leaf" variegated light green and dark; white flowers. Grows low.

'Thrush.'—See 'Robin.'

FOR ADVANCED GROWERS

'Alfreana'—Bushy type with pointed leaves silvery-gray enlivened with a fleecy effect from their downy white coating. Center starts dark Oxford-gray, follows veins in pattern halfway to leaf edge. Pearly pink flowers fairly frequent and abundant.

'American Beauty'—Lavish, bushy, upright grower with maple-shaped leaves in indescribable shades of lustrous red touched with black.

'Baby Rainbow'—Jewel-like miniature with round leaves, pointed tip; texture delicately crinkled. Rainbow of glowing color starts with bias-binding edge of royal purple; moves to wider band of basic green almost obscured by polished silver; to oval center of raspberry overlaid on amethyst. Not the easiest, but unquestionably one of the most glittering, rexes. Keeps its teacup size.

'Bearded'—Dusky-hued leaves in shades of green; darkest band around the edge. Rose-red "beard" stands out on leaves and stems, each hair bending at a geometric angle. Large waxed pink flowers.

'Bertha McGregor'—Past-century hybrid with large maple leaves olive-green, splattered and splotched with silver. Not the most brilliant, but stately and distinctive.

'Black Knight'—Properly, this name is a synonym for 'Midnight.' But in the East two distinctly different beauties are available under two names. This one is sheer, softest velvet of near-black maroon with a regular band of small bright pink dots over green one third of the way in from the margin. A dark, luscious beauty.

'Bronze King'—Large leaf with pronounced spiral, changeable bronze and green, tufts of hair from centers of tiny pink dots.

'Burvel'—Green leaves with red veins, stems, and edge thickly upholstered with red hair.

'Captain Nemo'—Distinct bands of green and silver-green, darker rim around the edge. Prominent spiral.

'Cardoza Gardens'—Heavy-textured, large leaf with gay fiesta colors

—red, silver, green—blood-red on the back. Red veins have heavy red hair. One of the brightest rexes.

'Carmelita'—Large dark green leaf with splotchy silver band, spiraled at the stem, tapering pointed at the tip; red hairs on stems and veins.

'Coon's Eye'—Silvery leaf with wavy edge; pearly toward the center. Upright habit.

'Countess Louise Erdoedy'—Credited as the first fully spiraled rex leaf. Coarse-textured silver-gray leaf studded with pink hairs, and flushed rose.

'Dewdrop'—Sheer, thin, ivy-shaped leaves completely inlaid with mother-of-pearl, which shimmers lavender-pink. Dwarf grower. Finicky about warmth; susceptible to mildew.

'Filigree'—Large, strong leaf with deeply cut "fingers," alternately marked with ebony and pink. Over-all effect is brilliant pink-splotched purple.

'Fire Flush,' or 'Bettina Rothschild'—Outstanding old-timer has never been imitated or equaled. Green leaves with red center zone and edge glimmer under a veil of finest red hairs—an indescribable effect. Unfolding new leaves so thickly silky-haired as to look like Gay Nineties plush. Fragrant white flowers.

'Helen Lewis'—Silky, tender leaf, royal purple in the center and on the edge, separated by a bold band of antique silver.

'Huntington Lake'—Large, spiraled leaf, pewter and lichen-green.

'Kathleyana'—Soft, star-pointed leaves, basically dark green, but thickly silver-dotted, except at the veins. Upright, branching type.

'Little Pet'—Pink and white luster on silver taffeta, veins and edge forest-green. Low grower with many medium-sized leaves.

'Marion Louise'—Pointed-edged leaf with green zone at the center and thin green rim at the edge, the area between smooth, silvery green or aquamarine.

'Modesty'—Elongated leaf soft green, self-spotted in a lighter silvery shade. 'Improved Modesty' is strong, colored pink and silver.

'Oregon Sunset'—Spiraled leaves look crinkled, crumpled— in glowing colors of a hardwood forest lit up by an autumn sunset.

'Pacific Sunset'—Aptly named for the horizonal colors as the sun sinks—soft, bright red, silver, with a plum glow.

'Pansy'—Dwarf with pointed dark green leaves, well-defined zone of lighter metallic green.

'Patsy'—Strikingly zoned, medium-size leaf in near black, silver, rose, and violet.

'Peacock'—Medium, round, brilliant black and scarlet leaves hug tight to the pot. Fertilize only sparingly, to keep the plant small and compact.

'Queen of Hanover'—Emerald plush banded with silver, ruby on the edge; mysteriously smoky under a film of fine light rose hairs.

'Red Berry'—Miniature with sheer leaves a solid shade of rich wine —like shimmering satin.

'Red Wing'—Tapering pointed leaves with wine-red center, silver edge, crimson tone over all.

'Silver Fleece'—Silky-haired, soft green leaves stippled with silver. Low grower.

'Star Dust'—Larger, slate-green leaves, thickly silver-dusted. 'Curly Star Dust' is the spiraled, ruffled form. 'Purple Star Dust' adds a violet undertone. 'Purple Curly Star Dust' has everything—pebbly texture, spiral, purple cast.

'Twisty Spot'—Medium leaf with distinct spiral, many points, ruffled edge; blending bands of varying red-bronze and green; raised silver spots, each with a red hair in dead center.

FOR COLLECTORS

'Annie Robinson'—Middle-sized, bushy type with roundish leaves, dark gray around a metallic center, deep red underneath.

'Avila'—Changeable-colored spiraled leaf rose, silver, green; center, a dark accent.

'Black Diamond'—Silver-freckled leaves of black-red with center zone of pewter. Restrained grower with upright tendencies.

'Calico'—Medium-sized plant, leaves about six by ten inches. Center and edge, purple-black, green zone between; completely covered with silver polka dots which turn lavender in strong light. No two leaves exactly alike. There is a spiraled 'Curly Calico.'

'Curly Fire Flush'—Spiral version of the old-timer, more temperamental.

'Curly Mulberry'—Spiraled leaf with sharp bands of purple and silver.

'Emerald Giant'—Large, pointed leaf, rich green with bands of tan to brown.

'Emperor'—Large leaf, neither striped nor patterned, light green and pimpled, with iridescent lavender effect.

'Evergreen'—Among all the jewel-hued rexes, this one stands out for its luxuriant leaves of solid woodsy green. Texture of the finest, silkiest.

'Glory of St. Albans'—Brilliant but temperamental diva with thin, tender leaves, changeable rose, violet, and silver; distinct border like intricately braided metallic floss.

'Her Majesty'—Tapering velvet leaf in Oriental tones of jet and frosted pink.

'His Majesty'—Sheer velvet in royal hues: garnet, silver, purple.

'Indian Summer'—Extremely large, lavishly ruffled leaf of forest-green with wide zone of Indian-red.

'Lord Palmerston'—Gay Nineties favorite with soft leaves banded in varying tones of green.

'Louise Closson'—One of the brilliant but difficult 'Closson' rexes. Blood-red miniature leaf with metallic sheen, tender texture.

'Lucille Closson'—Typical, brilliant 'Closson'-type dwarf with black-red leaves splotched purplish-pink.

'Lucy Closson'—Bronzy 'Closson' leaf flecked with purple and pink; delicate dwarf.

'Midnight'—Large, textured, smoke-gray leaf dusted with fine white pinpoints. See 'Black Knight.'

'Mikado'—Sheer velvet leaf; royal-purple center and narrow edge; lustrous silver-green between.

'Mohegan'—Small leaves glow red-rose with edge of blackish "binding."

'Mountain Haze'—Deep rose, silver-dusted, soft leaf with a cloudy or smoky sheen.

'Mrs. A. G. Shepherd'—Erect, with basically bright green leaves inlaid with silver, except on the edges.

'Mrs. H. G. Moon'—Upright and branched. Sparse-hairy leaves stippled with several shades of green and silver, and lavender-flushed.

'Mulberry'—Brown and silver zones with an intoxicating mulberry sheen.

'Nigger Tree'—Upright type needs pinching to keep compact. Velvety leaves, midnight-green, with band of grass-green.

'Ojai'—Spiraled leaf of medium size, bumpy texture, fluted edge—in an incomparable combination of rich green, silver, violet.

'Perle de Paris'—Nubby "elephant-ear" leaves, changeable silver-green; canary-yellow flowers.

'President'—Also listed as 'Carnot' or 'President Carnot.' Large, dusky green leaves heavily blotched with silver. Usually holds its leaves through winter. Spiraled form is 'Curly Carnot.'

'Prince Charming'—Richly textured, round-pointed leaf—as if an artist laid on a basic dark green tone, then stippled thick silver dots between the veins, added the final fairy-tale touch of a pink flush.

'Princess of Hanover'—Identical with 'Queen of Hanover' except for the gracious, graceful spiral.

'Scarlet O'Hara'—Two different plants appear with this name. One is a plain, dark red leaf. At the Montreal Botanical Gardens, it is colorfully spotted with brightest pink.

'Silver Greenheart'—Large silver leaves feathered green along the main veins.

'Solid Silver'—Large, monotoned silvery-green leaves and attractive porcelain-like flowers.

'Sunburst'—Gray-green metallic leaf, fleetingly pink-suffused, with dark green sunburst radiating out from the stem; silver-spotted dark green border; large, to twelve inches, and doubly spiraled.

'Van-Ex'—Many- and large-leaved plant of upright habit; leaves, textured silver on green.

REXES TO WATCH OR WAIT FOR

'Autumn Colors'—Miniature. Small leaves have dark red centers shading to brown, partly overlaid with silver.

'Charlotte Hoak'—Large, spiraled green leaf with red-haired and ruffled edge.

'Edna Korts'—New variety with large, doubly spiraled leaves.

'Joel Gillingwators'—Vigorous grower to great size; leaves neatly patterned all along the veins and on the edge.

'Purple Heart'—Upright type. Thin, delicate, transparent leaves purplish-black and blue, contrasting zones of silver, flushed reddish-purple. Somewhat difficult, but outstandingly handsome.

'Sonie'—Large, smooth leaf in an artful pattern of silver and dark green, with red-green veins. Gently ruffled on the edge. New.

'Winter Queen'—Hardy winter grower and bloomer. Glistening silver leaf, deeply spiraled, sharply marked with purple on the edge and in center zone, all with a rosy lavender overtone. Pink flowers show well above foliage.

Odd and Rare Begonias

Come into this "curiosity shop" and get acquainted with some of the most unusual—and unusually lovely—plants ever discovered along treacherous jungle trails, clinging to mountain crags, or cultivated by tropical tribesmen. These are for the daredevil grower who fancies the unusual, the "offbeat," and is willing to invest extra time in fulfilling this fancy. Most are frankly difficult to grow outside a greenhouse, and sometimes inside.

Some of these begonias are more odd than beautiful; others combine rare beauty with impossible cultural demands; some are both rare and lovely, and can be grown with reasonable assurance of success. Each one is an individual delight—with its own individual ideas about how it likes to grow.

If there are any principles for growing and propagating these odd and rare begonias, they are the rules outlined in Chapters 3 and 4, and they are only a starting point. From these, you may take off in all directions. Delicate *cathayana,* for example, requires more warmth and humidity than most exotic orchids. Succulent *venosa* should be grown as warm and dry as a cactus. Velvety *griffithi* had best be kept in a terrarium. You'll find some specific tips in the varietal descriptions; you can probably get more from the grower of your rare begonia. Add your own quota of patience and common sense, and you're likely to succeed.

NAMED VARIETIES OF ODD AND RARE BEGONIAS

Here are a few varieties which are readily available and not too difficult to grow; more for the advanced grower, and the collector; and some exciting new treasures to covet when they are made available.

FOR BEGINNERS

epipsila (Brazil)—Thick, polished, leathery green leaves coated with red-brown wool underneath. Grows low; droops attractively. Showy ovaries on white flowers.

evansiana (China)—Named for collector's employer, Evans. Popularly called the "hardy begonia"—but not truly hardy. Also called "tuberous"—actually bulbous. May survive a New York City winter with care and protection. Can be wintered over indoors. Attractive semishade garden plant with typical lopsided begonia leaves; flowers, pink or white. Bulbils nestle in the fork where leaf stem and main stem meet, may be picked and planted, or left to grow in their own way when they fall on the soil below.

gracilis (Mexico)—Name means "slender, graceful." The "hollyhock begonia"—so called for its tallish stalks with rosy flowers nestled close. One of few begonias forming bulbils next to the stem.

'Grey Lady' (*incana* x *venosa*)—Resembles *incana,* but more vigorous and easier to grow. Round, succulent leaves frosted with light white down; flowers, white.

incana, or *peltata* (Mexico)—Names mean "hoary," or "peltate." White-felted, fleshy green leaves attached to the stem near the center, like a lily pad. Drooping white flowers in good measure. Grow dryish, and root stem cuttings the same.

'Luwalter' (*incarnata* x *mazae*)—Semirhizomatous upright type with fringed coppery maple-shape leaves, pink flowers. Plantlets appear on leaves and along stems, send down roots when leaf cutting is propagated in the usual manner.

manni (Africa)—Named for collector Mann. The "rose-leaf begonia" —impersonator with branches like climbing rose canes; leaves similar to the hybrid teas; unusual flowers without typical begonia ovaries, white with red streaks, and hugging tight to the stem. Delightful in baskets.

martiana (Mexico)—Named for collector Martius. Near-hardy "hollyhock begonia," larger and tougher than *gracilis.* Tolerates considerable sun. Tubers are oddly cream-colored, thin-skinned, and nearly round. Plant with the old stem scar on top. Gather bulbils in the fall, store cool and dry, plant early the next year. Stake well. Grow in brightest light for most compact shape.

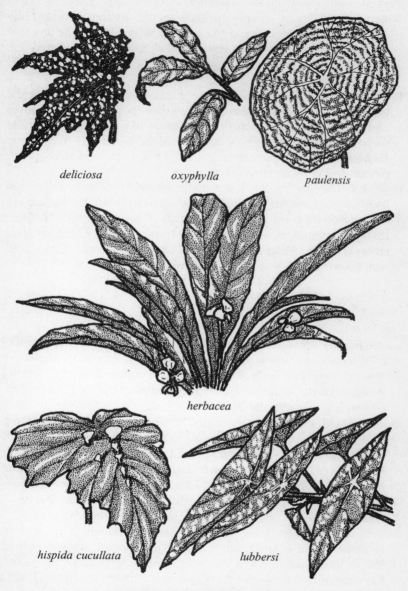

deliciosa *oxyphylla* *paulensis*

herbacea

hispida cucullata *lubbersi*

ODD AND RARE BEGONIAS

'Paul Bruant' (*heracleifolia longipila* x *frutescent*)—Large, straight stems; light green, deeply toothed leaves, lighter-veined. Fully opened pink flowers spread like a hoop skirt. One of the few that produce new plants on the stem, difficult to remove and grow on. Tip cuttings propagate most surely, or leaf cuttings with a sliver of main stem attached.

'Phyllomaniaca,' or 'Jessie'—Name means "crazy leaf." Upright grower with trunklike stems, glossy green, pointed leaves. Leaves and stems produce dozens of baby leaves like upstanding freckles which are difficult to grow into plantlets, but it has been done. Easiest propagation by stem cuttings. For a more shapely plant, put several cuttings in one pot.

woolly bear, or *leptotricha*—Latin name means "thin-hairy." Gnome-like "character actor" looks like a semp in a brown wool overcoat. Brown fuzz on shiny green leaf will rub off on your fingers. Leaves, thickish, cupped, close to stem. May branch, or may send up extra stems from the base. White flowers eagerly set seeds. Likes hard soil, growing dryish; blooms its head off.

FOR ADVANCED GROWERS

acida (Brazil)—Name means "sour, bitter." Large, seersucker-puck-ered leaves of freshest apple-green are round but seem angled by a suggestion of points where veins run out to the edge. Spring flowers dainty white on stems standing well above foliage. Pre-fers steady warmth and humidity.

aridicaulis (Mexico)—Name means "dry-stemmed." Lilliputian imp tries to grow up, but weak stems bend down, keeping total height under six inches. Terrarium gem. Little light green, fingernail-sized leaves flutter sharp points under unusual two-petaled white flowers like winter snowdrops. This charmer barely escaped obli-vion when it first came to this country. The stems looked dry, dead, and hopeless, but were reborn in a propagating bench.

bartonea, or *winter jewel* (Puerto Rico)—Coquettish miniature branches freely, and dangles small, scalloped, russet-mottled leaves that glisten, when the light is right, with heavenly silver. Clusters of fine fairy-like flowers dance daintily in winter. Insists on warmth. Will collapse at the suggestion of a chill.

cooperi (Costa Rica)—For discoverer Cooper. Elm-shaped leaves on short, hairy stems; tightly bunched flowers.

diadema (Borneo)—Name means "two-crowned." Leaves cut too deeply to make a star, not deep enough to be palmlike; lustrous, silky bright green with tiny silver smoke rings between the veins. Unusual hidden underground rhizome. Flowers pink in fall. Heat- and moisture-lover.

'Gilsoni'—Named for Gilson, grower's gardener. Hybrid with crisp, half-folded triangular green leaves fringed with finest hair up and down; sturdy stalks, white-haired on the back. May be the only fibrous-rooted begonia, except for the semps, with double male flowers—four outer pink petals surround a center puff of pink petal-like (petaloid) shells. Likes warmth.

goegoensis (Sumatra)—Named for Goego, Sumatra. Lily-pad leaves, leathery bronze-green, corrugated by crisscrossing lighter green veins. Stems, square; flowers, pink. Grows warm.

'Perle Lorraine' (*polyantha* x *strigillosa*)—Oval-pointed leaves, apple-green overlaid with rich brown lace; underside, marbled green and red; flowers, peach-pink. Grows upright but keeps compact.

'Templini' (sport of 'Phyllomaniaca')—Tall green-and-yellow variegated version of the "crazy-leaf begonia," slightly more demanding of humidity and warmth; shows its best color and mottling in all but the brightest sun. Baby plants on the leaves have been rooted, but often revert to plain green color. Leaf-stem cuttings will propagate, but should be taken with the most colorful leaves to insure variegation in the new plant. Tip cuttings are easiest, but plants must never be cut all the way back.

vellozoana (Brazil)—Named for botanist Vellozo. Name is unfortunately similar to another begonia not grown now (*velloziana*). This is a recently introduced, sensational species with dark green taffeta leaves accented by light veins and an ethereal pink tinge. Pure white, pink-haired flowers on tall spikes. Not difficult from seed. Roots at the stipules, so leaf-stem cuttings with attached sliver of main stem are recommended.

FOR COLLECTORS

cathayana (China)—Named for Cathay. An antique Oriental queen. Silky velvet leaves zoned ruby-red and emerald-green; reversed underneath—glowingly rich when light shines through. Rare orange flowers. Requires warmth, protection from drafts, high humidity. Avoid sunlight and shocking with cold water. May drop some leaves when resting. Propagates from seeds, leaf-stem cuttings, tip cuttings.

cathcarti (India)—For English botanist Cathcart. Large, thick, cordate leaves, bristly hairs on stem when grown cool. Flowers deep yellow on long stems. Needs humidity.

chivatoa (Mexico)—For Mexican mountain. Ladylike, spinach-green leaves have veins so red-bearded on the underside as to look hoydenish. Foliage tips the thick branches. Winter bloomer, carmine. Soak thoroughly, then dry out completely before rewatering. Water sparsely during late-winter dormancy, from which it may or may not revive.

deliciosa (Borneo)—Name means "delicious." Upright, branched, with an untypical rhizome-like stem which hides just beneath the soil surface. Nicknamed "Indian-spotted" for the area of its origin and the ponderous gray spots on its olive-drab, deeply slashed leaves. Surprisingly large and lovely soft pink flowers.

dichotoma (Venezuela)—Name means "forked, two-branched." Treelike plant with brown stems becoming trunklike with age. Large, angular green leaves; small pearly white flowers.

dipetala (a variety of *malabarica*)—May be listed as 'Mrs. W. S. Kimball.' Latin name means "two-petaled." Flat, round leaf has red-inkspot where the stem ends; indented red veins give a corrugated effect. Hugging close to the stem, two-petaled pink flowers hang like heavenly pennies. Demands humidity and warmth.

froebeli (Ecuador)—Was collected for Froebel & Co., Swiss growers. Tuberous species that blooms in winter. Velvety pearl-gray leaves; fleshy red flowers like valentine hearts. Not difficult from seed, but hard to hold over after flowering. Keep tuber in soil in pot, or store in dry sand or vermiculite. Grows cool.

gigantea (India)—Name means "giant." Two- to three-foot species with a swollen base sending up many tall, slim stems topped by green, wing-shaped leaves, tipped by tight balls of flowers. Resembles a bird poised for flight.

griffithi (India)—Named for English botanist Griffith. Recently re-identified as species *annulata*. Fairy-tale miniature best suited for a terrarium. Leaves soft as silky peach down, in ruby, emerald, and rosy bands. Demands protective warmth and humidity.

hemsleyana (China)—Named for Hemsley of Kew Gardens. Shiny green leaflets radiate from stem end like umbrella ribs; flowers, precious pink. Propagate by stem cuttings. Leaves will produce viviparous plants.

hispida cucullata—Lobed, downy-soft leaves with upstanding adventitious leaflets marching along the veins; white flowers. Propagate by stem cuttings, or grow plantlets.

inflata (India)—Name means "swollen"; refers to seed pods. Stiff, sparsely branched stems support large elephant-ear leaves of an odd shade of green, with a queer sleazy-silk texture.

kenworthyi (Mexico)—Named for begonia personality Eva Kenworthy Gray. Leaves textured, shaped, and veined like the ivy, but more gray or powder-blue than green. Gnarled, scarred rhizome erect. Prefers more sun, less water than the average. When resting after bloom, keep warm and dry until new growth appears.

luxurians (Brazil)—Name means "luxuriant." Leaf like a small-scale palm, fuzzy and limp. Plant is few-branched, hard to flower. Propagation by stem tip cuttings has been known to kill the plant. Best chance is new growth from the bottom, after resting period, rooted with bottom heat.

olbia (Brazil)—Named for Olbia, Russia. Maple-shaped leaf of rich, lustrous, pale green satin-velvet; veins, darker; edge and underside, red. Erect and somewhat branched. Provide protective warmth, high humidity. Flowers, white.

paulensis (Brazil)—Shiny round green leaves spiderwebbed by crisscrossed veins, like sheer seersucker. Creamy white flowers with dark, wine-colored hairs. Grows well in sphagnum, or lightest soil mix. Keep warm and humid.

quadrelocularis, or *egregia* (Brazil)—First name refers to four-winged ovary. Woody, tree-type plant with long, tapering, pointed pebbly green leaves drooping neatly from both sides of the stem; flowers like tiny pink-tipped hearts, with uncharacteristic four-winged ovaries. Propagate from seeds, side shoots, or tip cuttings.

valdensium (Brazil)—Grass-green "elephant ear" leaves clean and clearly marked with lightest green veins which meet in a sparkling eye.

venosa (Brazil)—Name means "veiny." Incredibly frosty-felted, thick green cupped leaves, scented white flowers, and juicy stems wrapped around with thin brown tissue-paper stipules. This plant seems to shun water in soil or on leaves. Grows nearly as dry as cacti, in soil nearly as sandy, with nearly as little fertilizer but almost as much sun. Reportedly not easy to propagate, but it can be done if tip cuttings are kept quite dry. Also can be divided. Not a brancher, but sends up new growth from the base.

versicolor (China)—Miniature terrarium jewel of finest silk velvet; three-inch leaves toned mahogany, emerald, silver, apple-green, maroon. Flowers, salmon-pink.

VARIETIES TO WATCH OR WAIT FOR

crispula (China)—Unique species with silk-corded, gray-green leaves tight to the soil. Delicate and precious; requires careful watering, so tight-touching leaves won't rot.

herbacea (Brazil)—Epiphytic (grows on trees) plant with light green, silver-spotted leaves consistently shaped like the hart's-tongue fern. Flowers, white.

lubbersi (Brazil)—Silver-splashed dark leaves with the rare look of *Caladium humboldti;* stem attached near the middle of the leaf, which is pointed at both ends. Exotic.

philodendroides (Mexico)—A curiosity, with leaves like *Philodendron dubium*—smooth, leathery, deeply lobed; large white flowers; underground tuber-like rhizome; five to six months of dormancy out of the twelve. At the Montreal Botanical Gardens, after flowering, this plant looked ragged as it prepared to rest. It is not fed or repotted at this time, but in spring, when the rhizome starts fresh growth. This is connected to the old rhizome only by a narrow link. New leaf and flower stems come up through the soil.

rigida (Brazil)—Graceful tree type with umbrella-like leaves, blood-red ribs; halo-like hairs exalt pleated young leaves.

sulcata (Colombia)—Name means "furrowed." Brittle, crinkly-leaved dwarf with white flowers.

teuscheri (Malay)—Named for collector Teuscher, uncle of the Curator of the Montreal Botanical Gardens. Not an angel-wing. The correct species is not known to be in general cultivation today.

WINTER-FLOWERING TUBEROUS BEGONIAS
TOP ROW: 'Man's Favourite,' 'Lady Mac,' 'Exquisite.' MIDDLE ROW:
'John C. Mensing,' 'Pink Perfection,' 'Lady Roberts.' BOTTOM ROW:
'Snowdrop,' 'Emily Clibran,' 'Marietta.'

CHAPTER 14

Winter-Flowering Tuberous Begonias

Here come the Christmas begonias, the flower-smothered florist plants that make such impressively lovely holiday and winter gifts. Like small-scale replicas of the garden's summer-blooming tuberous begonias, these are flamboyantly colorful, with masses of showy flowers over large, round, gay green leaves.

There are two types of winter-flowering tuberous begonias, both descendants of the species *socotrana,* but each the result of a different cross. The *hiemalis* ("winterly") begonias—largest, lustiest, and most lavish in bloom—are offspring of *socotrana* and some tuberous species from the Andes. The *cheimantha* (from the Greek for "winter-flowering") begonias—smaller single flowers in shades of pink or white—are children of *socotrana* crossed with the African tuberous species, *dregei.* Both types flower in winter but do not necessarily go completely dormant in summer.

Begonia socotrana (for its home, the Indian Ocean's Island of Socotra) bestowed some very dominant characteristics upon both branches of its family tree: the characteristic rounded leaf shape with scalloped edge; the winter-blooming habit; the flower type. The small nut-sized tubers of *socotrana* are sometimes available today in early fall. The five- to eight-inch tuber clusters should not be separated, but kept intact and started into growth when green streaks appear, by the same method as for starting summer-flowering tubers in spring. Pot the well-rooted clusters of tubers when top growth is well established, and repot as growth progresses. Avoid rot-inviting overhead watering, which makes puddles where the leaves cup at the stem end. Grow fairly warm, moist, and humid, with all available deep-winter sun.

THE CHEIMANTHAS

In the old days, these "Christmas begonias" were often called "Busy Lizzie," or "Lorraine-type," for the first hybrid of the series, 'Gloire de Lorraine.' Nowadays you may hear the term "Scandinavian" or "Norwegian" begonias—for a new, improved, sturdier-stemmed strain of some outstanding varieties.

The bushy, full, well-branched plants have an abundance of large, rounded, clear green leaves, and literally hundreds of bright white or pink single flowers. Because the flowers are single, they're lighter and hold longer on the stems than the *hiemalis. Cheimanthas* also have a longer blooming season—November to Easter—and are somewhat easier to grow in the home.

To keep a gift *cheimantha* at the height of its beauty for as long as possible, keep it cool (70° by day, 60° by night) in draft-free, humid, but fresh air—the soil constantly moist, but not soggy. Give it plenty of light and some sunlight, but don't let the sun's rays concentrate through window glass to burn leaves and flowers.

When flowering is finished, you may want to grow the plant on for bloom the following winter. This is not too easy, but it is also not impossible. Cut back the plant severely; continue to keep it cool and moist; and watch for new shoots coming up from the base. These may be cut off and rooted when they have two or more nodes. Provide propagating-box protection.

Professional growers propagate *cheimanthas* from leaf cuttings taken with some stem, which are rooted early in the year, after flowering. Either kind of cutting roots best in humid air, but will rot or mildew easily if either air or the propagating medium is kept too wet.

Named Varieties

The new "Scandinavian" group includes: rose-pink-flowering 'Carolina,' deep rose 'Marina,' cerise 'Red Solfheim,' dark pink 'Solbakken,' red 'Spirit of Norway,' and rich rose 'Tove.'

The original 'Gloire de Lorraine' (*socotrana* x *dregei*) is still popular, with pink flowers—and so are some of the other old-timers, such as rose-flowered 'Marjorie Gibbs' and soft pink 'Melior.'

'Lady Mac' is the variety most widely available, and perhaps one of the least finicky growers. It is offered with either pink or white flowers. Many list this or similar varieties simply as "Christmas White" or "Christmas Pink" begonia.

'Gloire de Sceaux' (*socotrana* x *subpeltata*) is not properly a *cheimantha,* because of its different parentage. But it is similar in appearance and requires similar culture. It has large rose flowers over iridescent dark bronzy leaves.

THE HIEMALIS

These winter-flowering tuberous or semituberous hybrids have showy double flowers or dogwood-like single flowers up to four inches across, in shades of pink, red, white, and in-between salmon and apricot. You may see or hear these referred to as "Clibran begonias," for the Holland firm which originated one of the finest strains. Later developments and improvements have come from the House of Baardse.

These plants may look lustier, but they are even more brittle and touchy than *cheimanthas* about how they grow. They like cooler air —between 55° and 60°. They resent water on their leaves, are more susceptible to mildew and rot, and are even more difficult to propagate.

After flowering, you may save the plant for next year by placing it where it can keep cool (50° at night) and keeping the soil neither wet nor dry, but slightly moist. When the tops die down, part of the old stem may remain. Hang up a "Don't Disturb" sign until late March. Then, shake off the soil around the tuber and start it afresh in a smaller pot. Cuttings may be taken when new shoots have one or more nodes. Disinfect cut ends, and insert in propagating box or some other humidifying device.

At replanting time, old plants can be divided by separating clusters containing at least five of the bulbils found near the soil surface.

Professionals propagate *hiemalis* begonias by leaf-stem cuttings, often with a small heel or sliver of the main stem attached to the leaf stem, taken in November or December. By March, small tubers are formed and new growth is coming up from them. The new plants are kept cool in summer (65°) and are pinched out regularly until mid-August, to increase branching.

Named Varieties

'Altrincham Pink'—Fully double rosebud flowers, deep pink, through Christmas. One of the first Clibran hybrids, still a stand-by.

'Apricot Beauty'—Double deep apricot flowers.

'Baardse's Wonder'—One of a beautiful new strain with braggart single flowers of deep velvety red, and enlarged black stamens that look like auxiliary petals.

'Emily Clibran'—Popular beauty with double salmon-pink flowers.

'Emita'—Single copper-salmon flowers.

'Exquisite'—Dogwood-type flowers, large, single, glowing pink.

'Fairy'—Delicate semidouble pink.

'Flambeau'—Double salmon-red flowers.

'John C. Mensing'—Dwarf type with orange flowers.

'Lady Roberts' ('Princess Irene,' or 'Mrs. Roberts')—Double flowers in old ivory.

'Man's Favourite'—Three- to four-inch single white dogwood flowers.

'Marietta'—Large double apricot.

'Nellie Visset'—Double scarlet.

'Optima'—Early Clibran hybrid, single orange-pink.

'Pink Perfection'—Double rosebud-pink.

'Rosalind'—Single deep pink.

'Rose Queen'—Semidouble rose suffused with red.

'Snowdrop'—Fully double heavenly white.

'The Pearl'—Double creamy white.

'The President'—Double red.

'Vander Meer's Glorie'—Single orange.

CHAPTER 15

Summer-Flowering Tuberous Begonias

Brilliant . . . glorious . . . magnificent—these are some of the more restrained adjectives bestowed on a garden display of tuberous begonias in full flower. Growers act like addicts, speak of them in hushed tones. Enthusiasts often even forget that these are not the only members of the begonia family; to them, "begonia" is merely a shortened version of "tuberous begonia."

The summer-flowering tuberous begonias (properly collected under the group name, *tuberhybrida*) provide the longest season of the largest and showiest flowers—in the most superlative range of colors—of any bedding plant, bar none. And they reach and keep this peak in places where sunlight is too scarce for most annuals, perennials, and shrubs to bloom.

Except for species, which are mostly grown in pots by collectors, there are three general types of summer-flowering tuberous begonias. Today's *tuberhybrida* are complicatedly intercrossed hybrids, bred for ever-larger and more perfectly formed flowers on sturdier plants and stems. *Multiflora* is a group of smaller, more compact plants with a superabundance of smaller flowers. *Pendula* types have a trailing and hanging habit, and make gorgeous displays in baskets.

All three types take similar culture, and serve similar decorative purposes. Each has its own individual personality and its own devotees. All are the remote offspring of one or more tuberous-begonia species seldom seen, except in collections.

THE TUBERHYBRIDA

Blooming with reckless abandon in all colors except blue, these tuberous begonias are most often used en masse or in rows in outdoor garden beds. Or single potted specimens may be grouped to decorate patio, terrace, or porch. Or they're cultivated for the spectacular impression they make in competition or exhibition. Their cut

165

flowers make exotic corsages, flower arrangements, and table decorations.

Modern varieties have been bred with two goals in mind—tremendous flowers (sometimes up to eight or ten inches across) of perfect color and form; and disease-resistant plants with stems sturdy enough to hold such heavy flower heads high. Tubers are more frequently catalogued according to flower form, rather than named varieties in endless variation. Each year, hybridists announce some new achievement. In 1959, one sensation was the rose form beginning to emerge from the ruffled-camellia type. Next year, and in the years after that, more and more perfect beauty is a promise.

Types of Flower Form

This is a composite classification based on the American Begonia Society's *tuberhybrida* classes in their annual competitive show, plus listings in growers' catalogues.

Camelliaeflora (camellia type, camellia-flowered, double camellia-flowered). Flowers are breathtakingly beautiful, fully double, in all typical colors, and incredibly large—up to ten inches in diameter. Because the larger petals are fewer than in other double forms, the flowers are not too heavy to be supported by the stems. Resemblance to the corsage camellia is pronounced.

Ruffled camellia (double-ruffled camellia). Camellia-type blooms with petals swirled, frilled, fluted, or ruffled on the edge—looking less like real camellias and more like a Southern belle's hoop skirt. One registered trade-mark for American ruffled double hybrids is 'Ballerina.' Another group of outstanding varieties schematically uses names like 'Santa Barbara,' 'Santa Maria,' and other 'Santas.'

Fimbriata plena (carnation-flowered, double-carnation type). Flowers have many petals with saw-toothed edges—so many, in fact, that breeders have kept flower size under an eight-inch diameter so the blooms are not too heavy for the stems to hold.

Cristata (crested). Flowers are big, buoyant, single, and distinguished by a tufted crest on each of four petals, somewhat like a cockscomb. They are available in a full range of colors.

Crispa undulata (single-frilled, *crispa* types). Gigantic, showy single flowers; petal margins crisply frilled.

Narcissiflora (daffodil-type). Flowers are neither showy nor plenteous, but are often fragrant, and excite interest for their resemblance to giant daffodils.

Marginata. Flowers come in two forms. *Double marginatas* are double flowers with each petal veined and edged with a thin, precise line of a contrasting color. *Crispa marginatas* are frilled singles with the same edging. The markings are similar to picotee, but in heavier bands.

Marmorata. A bicolor form of the camellia type, with slightly smaller rosy flowers streaked with bright white. 'Stars and Stripes' is a well-known variety.

Picotee. The term for petals outlined on the edge with an irregular border of another color, which bleeds softly down into the dominant shade. Picotees are available in both camellia and rose form, and are being bred in other upright types, plus the hanging basket varieties.

Rosebud (horticultural group name, *Bouton de Rose*). Should not be confused with the newer, rose-form types. When rosebud flowers begin to open, the center petals form a cone like the heart of a real rosebud.

Rose Form. A new development catering to popular eagerness for high-centered flowers. It is actually a further developed camellia-flowered form which each year looks less like a camellia and more like an unfurling rose. In wide-open flowers, the center is a rosebud-like crown of petals which stands out from those flared back at the outer edge.

Single-flowering forms. These, like a large wild rose unadorned by ruffles, colored borders, or crests, are not widely grown in this country, although they are prized abroad for their outsize, beautifully translucent petals.

Named Varieties

More often than not, leading hybridizers list *tuberhybrida* by flower form, with a choice of colors. Among the varieties listed by name are these:

'A. L. Berry'—Double yellow.
'Ballerina'—A group of double-ruffled hybrids.
'Black Knight'—Double deep crimson.
'Charmain'—Double pink.
'Flambeau'—Double orange-scarlet.
'Frances Powell'—Double pink.
'Harmony'—Blush-colored picotee, double.
'Mandarin'—Double salmon-orange.
'Ninette'—Double pale pink.
'Olympia'—Double crimson.
'Prelude'—Camellia rose.
'Rebecca'—Double pink.
'Red Admiral'—Double vermilion.
'Red Triumph'—Double red.
'Rhapsody'—Double salmon.
'Santa'—First name for a group of double ruffled giants such as 'Santa Barbara.'
'Stars and Stripes'—Rose-colored camellia flowers blotched with white.

THE MULTIFLORAS

These compact, twelve- to eighteen-inch plants are unsurpassed for profuse bloom and impressive masses of brilliant color. They are outstandingly effective in window boxes, for edging garden beds, or planted in front of the taller *tuberhybrida* to camouflage bare stems.

So plentiful are the single or semidouble flowers that the attractive slender-pointed green or bronzy leaves are often completely concealed. Since the flowers are small and light, they stand perkily upright on the stems.

Only recently have the *multifloras* begun to enjoy the popularity their hardiness and colorful beauty deserve. They are the easiest summer-flowering tuberous begonias to grow. They will flourish with more sun and less moisture than the *tuberhybrida,* and seldom need pinching or staking. Soil should be light and humus-rich; drainage should be good.

Naturally, these smaller plants grow from smaller tubers. Most varieties will come true from seed, which are inexpensive and easy to grow.

Recent breeding of *multifloras* with camellia-flowered *tuberhybrida* has originated a new strain called *multiflora maxima, grandiflora,* or *gigantea,* with larger flowers more predictably double, but still hundreds per plant.

Named Varieties
Some of these are available only as mature tubers, some only as seeds; and some are sold both ways.

'Copper Gold'—Double old gold on yellow, toned with carmine.
'Flamboyante'—Single scarlet.
'Goethe'—Single carmine.
'Heimat'—Single orange.
'Helene Harms'—Delightful soft canary yellow flowers, mostly double; leaves, clean blue-green.
'Homeland'—Single salmon-orange.
'Mme. Richard Galle'—Apricot; single.
'Rambouillet'—Semidouble red.
'Splendour des Tuileries'—Semidouble orange-salmon.
'Tasso'—Semidouble pink.
'William Eysser'—Semidouble deep salmon.

THE PENDULAS

The trailing tuberous varieties drip cascades of color from baskets hanging on porch or patio, glorify semishady window boxes, or run riot in rock gardens. Catalogues often list them simply as 'Lloydi' or "hanging basket begonias." Some suppliers list the species, *sutherlandi,* which has salmon-orange flowers and spear-shaped, delicate green leaves, occasionally red-veined. Among the modern hybrids, single flowers have now nearly given way to doubles, like miniature camellias, which shower down on all sides. Picotee types are an even newer innovation.

Exciting specimen plants are grown from the largest tubers, three to four years old, which produce the greatest number of branching stems. The *pendulas* are sensitive to excessive wind, sun, and moisture in both air and soil. They need warmth and humidity, feed voraciously on fertilizers and manure. Early in the growing season, hanging can be encouraged by pinching out the crown shoots, or by allowing the plants to wilt down just slightly in dry soil.

HOW TO GROW TUBEROUS BEGONIAS

Capsuled culture for all types of summer-flowering tuberous begonias includes: partial shade; cool, fresh air and free circulation; rich, light soil; perfect drainage; moisture in both air and soil. With some special care these varieties can be grown in short-summer areas such as Vermont or Minnesota; in the dusty dry heat of Kansas; even the salty air and stony gardens of the Maine coast.

Starting from Seeds

To make your work worth while, buy the best seeds available from the most reliable source. Usually, they will be listed by flower types and colors. Although the plants will not be so large or the bloom so heavy as with tubers, the cost is only fractional, and first-year seedlings usually bloom vigorously, with good-sized flowers.

Nature has made it possible for you to produce your own seeds, to increase your tuberous collection. Near the end of the summer, the showy double male flowers become smaller and single—and, in the process, are equipped with fertile pollen which can be used in pollinating female flowers, as outlined in Chapter 17. This fertile, single stage can be hurried by drying the plants prematurely. Hybridwise, of course, the new seedlings need not closely resemble either parent or both.

In long-summer areas, seeds are sown as early as January. Where spring comes late, February or March is safer, so the seedlings will not outgrow their quarters before they can be planted outside. Germination occurs within eight to thirteen days when seeds are kept moist, fairly cool (65°–70°), and in the dark. After one or two transplantings, when seedlings are four to five inches tall, they are ready to be set outside as soon as the weather is warm.

Selecting Tubers

Today's best varieties are sturdy plants with strong stems which will uphold many large flowers without staking; with some inbred resistance to disease, particularly mildew; and with tubers of good size. No matter what type of tuber you buy, growing the best requires the same space, work, and care as tubers of doubtful quality. Anything less than the best is no bargain at any price.

This summer's most vigorous and floriferous plants grow from tubers produced by seedlings started last year. Most tubers can and should be saved and regrown from year to year; but you should also try to start out on new varieties with the youngest, most vigorous plants available.

Tubers are usually size-graded from small one- or two-inch diameter (fine for outdoor bedding in masses) up to large three inches or more (for exhibition plants). Tubers to be pot-grown should measure one and a half inches or more. The larger the tuber, the larger the plant, and the more (but not larger or better) the flowers.

Starting Tubers

Many and varied are the recommended methods—all good, all subject to change as growers gain new experience. Here is one simple system.

In early spring, when tubers—newly received, or stored over from last summer—develop bright pink eyes, set them a half-inch deep (cupped, concave, or indented side up) in a light, airy medium such as coarse leaf mold, or equal parts of sharp sand and peat or leaf mold. Growers no longer recommend use of peat alone, or other materials which pack and keep soggy; they are an invitation to tuber rot.

Space the tubers generously in a flat, shallow box or tray, and place it in good light where the rooting medium can be kept moist, and the temperature is a coolish 60°–70°. Watch for the all-important root growth which develops around the tuber, particularly from the top. When the eyes have grown into good-sized shoots and the first two leaves are of equal size and development, pot the tubers a half-inch below soil surface in generous but not oversized shallow pots (one two-inch tuber to a six-inch pot, or three to an eight-inch pot). The soil should be light, porous, and friable; and the pot should contain a good layer of drainage material like pebbles or broken crock.

At potting time, decide whether to remove all but the *tuberhybridas'* strongest stalks, for larger flowers, or whether to leave several stems for smaller-flowered but graceful and fuller plants. Any stems cut off can be rooted and grown on. *Multifloras* and *pendulas* are grown and branch naturally when all stems and branches are left intact.

Grow the plants on in good light, at moderate temperature—re-

Flat of rooting tubers, all inserted at the same time. Some have hardly started; some have good-sized leaves and stems.

potting when the pots are root-filled—until warm weather permits outdoor planting. This warmth should be both by day and by night, not just a few mild hours on a sunny morning. If the plants develop too fast and furiously and become too large to handle before outdoor planting weather, they can be held back with cooler temperature. If they are growing too slowly, a warmer temperature will hurry them up.

Many growers do not preroot tubers indoors, but keep them in dark, cool storage until the weather warms up. If the shoots have not grown more than an inch or so long, they can be planted directly in the soil—and will produce first flowers only a week or two later than prestarted plants. This is a welcome laborsaver, if you can control storage conditions so the stems won't grow too long and the tubers won't rot.

GARDEN CULTURE

Granted, there are some areas where the climate is not naturally suitable for growing tuberous begonias—but very few where the word "impossible" applies. Heavy soil can be lightened; hot air can be cooled; dry air can be humidified; shade can be provided when sunlight is blistering. And few garden plants so richly reward the grower who makes the minimum effort to provide suitable growing conditions.

Temperature

Larger, more lasting flowers and more compact plant form are produced in cool summer air, or when the night air is sufficiently cool (55°–65°) to allow plants to recover from daytime heat. Where summer days and nights are extremely hot, the air can be cooled and humidity raised by frequent hosing with a fine mist (*not* when the sun is shining on the plants), or wetting down walks and nearby lawns. Where hot winds are prevalent, some sort of screen can be rigged up, with sheets or burlap, to protect the plants.

When tuber is ready to pot, roots grow from all sides; top growth is of good size.

Inevitably, temperature is tied up with humidity—and tuberous begonias like humid air. The cooler the air, the lower the humidity they will accept. With more heat, they require more moisture in the air.

Location

"Shade plant" is a misleading misnomer for these beauties. If grown in dense shade, they become tall and floppy, produce few flowers and leaves, and are easy prey to rot and mildew. They should be planted where they can enjoy two or three hours of early-morning and late-afternoon sun—on the north side of house or wall, or in the dappled shade of a high-branched tree—and where strong or hot winds won't dry the air and soil, or batter tender stems.

Soil

Good drainage is essential. If the soil is hard or claylike, lighten it with humus; improve drainage with sand; and raise the bed an inch or two, so rains can run through or off. Well-rotted manure can be dug in or used as a top dressing, but it should not touch stems or tubers.

Moisture and Humidity

When soil and air are too dry, buds will drop off without opening. When they are too moist, rot and mildew are likely to invade. On hot, dry, bright days, keep the soil moist and mist the plants as often as possible. On damp, dark days, withhold water.

Fertilizer

If the soil is sufficiently rich in plant nutrients, additional feedings should begin only when the first flower buds appear. Regular biweekly applications of weak solutions of soluble fertilizer—organic, chemical, or both—are preferable to less frequent applications of a stronger solution. A well-balanced diet produces deep green, firm-textured leaves which may or may not turn under slightly on the edge. A definite roll on the edge points to overfeeding; sickly yellow-green leaves usually indicate that the plants are starved.

Pinching and Pruning

Only the hanging types should be pinched out to encourage branching—and this, early in the season, before flower buds form. For larger flowers and better form on *tuberhybridas,* remove the buds of the female flowers (one on each side of the larger, center male) before they open. For mass color display, allow all buds to open naturally. And for late-summer exhibition flowers, remove all buds up to the end of June.

Staking, Grooming

Prize plants not only lose their prize-winning look but also court disease when faded leaves and flowers are not promptly removed. Staking individual flowers may be a nuisance, but it is a necessity when you've taken care to encourage large, showy flowers which are heavy on the stem.

If possible, place stakes when the tubers are first set out. If not, make sure the stake doesn't pierce the tuber or scar the stem. Tie stems loosely, to allow room for growth, with some soft material like raffia or strips of old nylon stockings.

Fall and Winter Care

Leaves turning dry and yellow, and large double male flowers becoming smaller and single, are signals that dormancy is approaching. Let up a little on watering, but let growth—particularly tuber development—continue as long as possible, at least until the time of the first light frost.

Dig tubers carefully, wash clean, and dry thoroughly, until the main stem falls off of its own accord or can be lightly disjointed with your hand. Dust the dry tubers with sulfur or powdered charcoal, and store in shallow, open trays or flats which permit free circulation of air. Keep cool (45°–50°), dark, and dry until rerooting time in spring. A root cellar, an unheated cellar where they will not freeze, or even the vegetable bin in a refrigerator are suitable storage places.

HOW TO PROPAGATE TUBEROUS BEGONIAS

You can increase your collection of identical plants for mass planting or exhibit by dividing tubers or taking stem cuttings. Protection of a prop box or something similar is a wise precaution until the progeny are well rooted and established, but neither rooting medium nor air should be kept dank and wet.

At summer's end, double male flowers turn single. Plants are dug, the tops dried, before storing.

Division

When pink sprouts begin to appear in spring, cut tubers cleanly into as many pieces as there are sprouts. Disinfect with sulfur or powdered charcoal and set the divisions aside to dry for several days, until the cuts are scarred over.

Plant divisions a half-inch deep in sharp sand; bottom heat will speed up rooting. When new plants are potted, fertilize sparingly. Removing the first set of flower buds will strengthen the small plant until it is strong and established.

Cuttings

These may be three-inch tips of new growth taken at almost any time, or three- to four-inch sprouts from tubers cut with a "basal ring" (a small, thin shield of tuber) attached. Trim off large leaves. Disinfect both cut tuber and stem end, and allow the cuttings to harden.

Sink stems in rooting medium; keep the temperature above 60°. In three to five weeks, when good roots have developed, pot and treat similarly to tuber divisions. These plants will usually produce small bulbs by fall and will flower exactly like the parent plant the following year.

FORCING FOR WINTER BLOOM

Thanks to two fairly new discoveries—the long-day versus short-day flowering principle, and growing under artificial light—summer-flowering tuberous begonias now glorify window sills and flower shows in winter. These plants are so constituted that they flower when daylight hours are long, go dormant when days are short. Artificial light for a full fourteen-hour day, or for four or more hours after twilight, provides the extra light they need to grow and flower.

Some dealers now store tubers under ideal conditions until October, when they can be rooted, potted, and flowered in spring or earliest summer. Summer-planted seedlings are also good subjects for forcing.

Or cuttings can be taken from outdoor plants in August, rooted, potted, and flowered with the aid of artificial light from November through April. These do not usually form tubers, and are too tired to continue healthy growth and bloom by the time summer rolls around again.

TUBEROUS BEGONIA SPECIES FOR COLLECTORS

Among these are the ancestors of modern summer-blooming tuberous hybrids. Many are not generally available or are not cultivated today. Some are true exotics with cultural idiosyncracies which are difficult to satisfy. A few, as noted, are available and amenable.

balmisiana—A cool grower with small, single pink flowers. Bulbils are produced where the leaf joins the main stem. May not be in cultivation now.

baumanni—Named for German plant specialist. Unusual species producing melon-size tubers in the wild; used as a food for animals. Large, rose-red flowers are delightfully fragrant. Grows cool and moist.

boliviensis (from Bolivia)—Tall, slender, distinguished *tuberhybrida* ancestor with clusters of five-petaled orange-scarlet flowers with golden stamens. Good for garden border backgrounds; requires staking. Available.

brevicaulis—Name means short-stemmed. Rarely lovely, puckered and patterned leaves; pink flowers. Occasionally seen in botanical gardens and collections.

bulbifera—Name means bulb-bearing. Nineteenth-century Mexican species.

cinnabarina—Name means cinnabar-red. Upright type with large vermillion flowers.

clarkei—Named for Major Clarke. Branching grower, flowers deep rose-red.

crinita—Name means hairy. Erect, branching; flowers rose-pink.

davisi—Named for collector Davis.—Compact plant with broad, dark green leaves, fiery flowers.

fulgens—Name means shiny. Dwarf and spreading, with pure red flowers.

micranthera—Name means small-flowering. Your choice of three rare varieties: *fimbriata* (fringed), apricot flowers; *foliosa* (leafy), white-flowered; *ventura,* apricot. Occasionally available from seed.

palmaris—Tall type with white flowers.

pearcei—Named for collector Pearce. A species, fairly widely grown today, which contributed yellow flowers and brown-shaded leaves to early and modern hybrids.

picta—Name means painted. Pebbly green leaf mottled with bronze and brighter green; pink flowers.

pleiopetala—Name means double-flowered. Tall white flowers.

polypetala—Name means many-petaled. Flowers, red.

rosaeflora—Flowers, soft rose.

unifolia—Name means one-leaved.—A curiosity with one flat leaf, sparse flowers.

veitchi—Named for grower Veitch.—Occasionally seen today; large vermilion flowers.

CHAPTER 16

Decorating with Begonias

The varied and colorful begonias are the answer to an interior decorator's dream. Foliage and flowers offer so many colors, in such an incredible range of patterns and textures. Sizes start at miniature and go on up to enormous. There are begonias to suit every decorating scheme, from Early American to the newest modern, and to fill every decorating purpose, from framing or filling a picture window to centering a taboret or coffee table, from grouping en masse to spotlighting a single specimen.

But, like any plants, begonias will reward you with all these virtues only when you give them good growing conditions. You can't move a magnificent plant from a warm, humid, light, and airy greenhouse to a dark, dry living-room corner and expect its beauty to last. Too soon, the leaves will brown and crisp on the edge; the stems will stretch out awkwardly in search of light; the plant will look limp and sickly. And there's nothing decorative about a dying plant.

You can, of course, discard the plant when it reaches this stage and buy another. But if your budget is small and your heart is big, there are other ways out. You can limit your begonia decorating to areas where they will have sufficient natural or artificial light, warmth, and humidity to keep them healthy. Or you can grow the plants in some separate area, like a porch or greenhouse, or under artificial light in the cellar, and bring out a few at a time for display. Plants can take turns coping temporarily with difficult conditions without severe adverse effect.

With this important principle in mind, think of the many ways begonias can brighten your home. A vase can be replaced with a brilliant rex. The bathroom window sill looks cheerful with a row of miniatures—which, by the way, appreciate the humidity created by running water. Under a light in your foyer, greet guests with a beautiful begonia. In the kitchen or breakfast nook, arrange gay flowering semps.

Or you can bank a fireplace with a background of evergreen boughs. In front, place a single specimen or a group of silver-leaved rexes.

Miniatures look more gemlike set inside a large brandy snifter or clear glass fish bowl; or on an upturned custard cup in the center of a water-filled platter or tray—the reflection doubles the beauty. So does a mirror behind a plant on a table or desk.

With artificial light, you can create more permanent decorations. Fit one shelf of a bookcase or corner cupboard with fluorescent tubes; line the shelf with a protective tray, to hold moist vermiculite or peat; and keep plants growing happily for months on end. A single plant set in a dark corner will last longer when spotlighted by a desk or reading lamp.

Or a portable "indoor greenhouse"—constructed on the principle of the Wardian case and fitted with fluorescent fixtures—can be either ready-made or constructed to fit into some selected corner or cupboard shelf. With these, it is particularly important to make sure that the amount of light is sufficient to keep the plants healthy.

Among other artificially lighted indoor installations are room dividers topped by planter boxes; small sunken "gardens" in the corner of a tiled entrance hall; even goldfish pools in the living room or playroom, banked by rows of begonias and other suitable plants.

You can combine begonias with many other types of plants—providing the others have the same preference for light, temperature, and humidity. The colorful group of gesneriads—African violets, episcias, gloxinias, achimenes—has, generally, the same cultural tastes as begonias. Many foliage plants are good subjects too—caladiums, self-heading philodendrons, peperomias, aralias, dieffenbachias, and other aroids. Some suitable vines are cissus, ivy, philodendron, and the wide variety of inch plants.

In your decorating, be imaginative and daring; dream up your own original ideas. Whatever the effect you strive for, there's a begonia that will help you achieve it. Select varieties for flower, form, color, texture, size. Use one large specimen as an accent, or a mass of colorful plants like a tapestry. Hang one basket begonia in a window, or put twins in attractive containers on the wall at each side. You have endless variations to work with.

VARIETIES FOR SPECIAL DECORATING PURPOSES

For Flowers

No matter where you put it, a plant in bloom is undeniably decorative. As a group, the *semperflorens* begonias will give you the most frequent and prolonged flowering periods throughout the year. The angel-wings will also bloom intermittently. And the blooming twins, 'Preussen' and 'Sachsen,' have racked up long periods of continuous flowering, even up to two years or more.

Other floriferous varieties are: 'Corbeille de Feu,' *fuchsioides,* 'Oadi,' 'Odorata Alba,' *scharffi, schmidtiana,* 'Tea Rose,' 'Viaudi.'

For flowers in fall and early winter, the *cheimanthas* are usually available at greenhouses and florists. Other varieties: *bartonea,* 'Digswelliana,' 'Drosti,' *hugelli,* 'Illustrata,' *incarnata,* 'Neely Gaddis,' 'Prunifolia,' 'Rosea Gigantea,' *subvillosa.*

Midwinter bloomers: *alnifolia,* 'Bessie Buxton,' 'Crestabruchi,' *dipetala,* 'Dorothy Grant,' *dregei,* 'E. O. Orpet,' *incana,* 'It,' *kellermanni,* 'Limminghei,' 'Luwalter,' *maculata,* 'Marjorie Daw,' 'Mrs. Fred D. Scripps,' *nitida,* 'Paul Bruant,' 'Phyllomaniaca,' *roezli, schulziana,* 'Templini,' 'Robin,' 'Viau-Scharff.' 'Weltoniensis.' And of course, the glorious winter-flowering *hiemalis* group.

Flowering in late winter and early spring are mature rhizomatous begonias, plus *venosa, convolvulacea,* and a few others.

For Small Plantings

There are many little begonias delightfully suitable for terrariums, miniature or dish gardens, and small Wardian cases. Among the rexes: 'Baby Rainbow,' 'Dewdrop,' 'Pansy,' 'Red Berry,' 'Black Diamond,' 'Lucille Closson.' The rhizomatous *boweri, hydrocotylifolia, rotundifolia, conchaefolia* will also stay small. Or choose *aridicaulis,* or tender *griffithi* or *versicolor.* Or use a brilliant young rex, and remove it when it grows ungainly.

For Accent

If you need a large specimen to stand out in a group, or to stand in stately splendor on the floor beside a chair, try one of the taller angel-wings; or rhizomatous 'Erythrophylla,' 'Ricinifolia,' 'Joe Hayden,' 'Ricky Minter,' *carolineaefolia,* 'Carol Star'; or hairy-leaved 'Mrs. Fred D. Scripps,' *scharffi;* or rex 'Fire Flush.'

For Texture

If your decorating idea calls for a touch of the soft and velvety, select one of the hairy-leaved varieties like 'Houghtoni,' *scharffiana, macrocarpa pubescens;* or *olbia, griffithi.* The lustrous *vellozoana* is silky; rex 'Can-Can' is like taffeta; 'Brocade,' 'Silver Star,' and 'Legacy' give a brocaded effect. 'Pebble Lane,' *iron cross, pustulata,* and many of the rexes have a rough, pebbly texture. Or there's the shiny, waxed gleam of the foliage of the semps, and others like *nitida,* 'Bunchi,' *longibarbata.*

For Specific Color

You can even select begonias which will work out a certain color scheme—and you'll find nearly every needed hue in flowers or foliage.

For shades of red, choose from: *macrocarpa pubescens,* 'Mme. Fanny Giron,' 'Thurstoni,' *sanguinea,* 'Shippy's Garland,' and rexes like 'Merry Christmas,' 'Red Berry,' 'Robin,' 'King Edward IV.'

White: *nitida,* 'Odorata Alba,' 'Skeezar'—and the white-flowering semps, angel-wings, *cheimantha,* or *hiemalis.*

Chartreuse: *iron cross,* 'Beatrice Haddrell,' 'Maphil' or 'Cleopatra,' 'Bow-Chancee,' *boweri, sunderbruchi,* 'Crestabruchi,' *dayi,* 'Virbob,' *pinetorum.*

Silver: 'Abel Carriere,' 'Sir Percy,' 'Zee Bowman,' *rubro-venia silver,* 'Silver Star,' and many rexes like 'Silver Sweet' and 'Solid Silver.'

Purple: 'Arthur Mallet,' 'Tingley Mallet,' 'Margaritacea,' 'Arabelle,' 'Gloire de Jouy,' and rexes like 'Helen Lewis,' 'Mikado,' 'Can-Can.'

Green: *acida, imperialis smaragdina, stitched leaf,* 'Verde Grande,' rex 'Evergreen,' and others.

This is only a beginning. From accenting a flower arrangement with a single brilliant rex leaf to filling a bay window or sun porch with small, medium, large, and trailing begonias, there are varieties for every decorative purpose.

CHAPTER 17

Name Your Own New Begonias

Beginner, collector, professional grower, or botanist—everyone can shine in this fascinating field. With all our thousands of beautiful begonias, we can still enjoy more and better varieties. The discovery or creation of even one—through lucky chance or patient, painstaking work—is a mighty satisfying experience.

New begonias come into cultivation by several different routes. Natural species are discovered and collected by dedicated botanists. The tales of their travels through tropical, snake-ridden swamps or to the tops of sheer, icy mountains read like an adventure story. The plants they have brought into cultivation are a rich horticultural treasure.

Chance seedlings are donated by bees and other insects which haphazardly fertilize flowers. A resulting seedling sometimes grows up to be just the kind of begonia the world has always wanted.

Nature contributes mutations, new variations on old species or hybrids. And man does the work of planned hybridizing—mating one begonia with another, to achieve some definite goal. No matter which way a new begonia originates, if it's really new and different, the plant world is richer, and its discoverer or creator has good reason to be proud.

MUTATIONS

Some people call them "sports." Mutations result from a spontaneous change in a plant's structure—usually in some portion of the plant, such as a branch. For example, the usually plain green leaves on one stem may suddenly become streaked and splashed with white (the calla-lily begonia is a mutation of a plain-leaved *semperflorens*) or yellow (cream-splotched 'Templini' is a mutation of crazy-leaved 'Phyllomaniaca').

A rhizomatous begonia with round, pond-lily-like leaves ('Erythrophylla') once, of its own accord, decided to dress up with a spiral, where stem meets leaf ('Erythrophylla Helix'). Much later, and on another plant, the spiraled leaves began to wave and crimp on the edges. That's how 'Bunchi' was born.

To complicate the picture and compound the elements of chance, 'Charm' is a chance seedling of a mutation, the calla-lily begonia.

If one of your begonias goes berserk with some new form of flower, leaf, or habit, what should you do? Cross your fingers and hope that Nature has given you a true mutation. First, make sure the new characteristic is not caused by some problem or pest; that it is prevalent on one branch or section of the plant, not just one leaf; and that, as far as you can find out, it has not appeared on the same variety at some other time and been christened by someone else.

So far, so good. Next, find out whether your mutation can be propagated—by cuttings, of course. You can't count on mutations to come true from seed. If a leaf, stem, or rhizome cutting will root and produce more plants with the same exciting new characteristics— you're in business. You have a brand-new begonia variety to be proud of.

In propagating, take special care with variegated mutations; they're often difficult to root. The white or creamy portion of the leaf lacks color because it lacks chlorophyll; and without chlorophyll it can't "digest" the nourishment a plant gets from sun, water, soil. In other words, it "has no stomach." Select cuttings with the greatest possible proportion of green in the leaves.

When they reproduce their new characteristics through propagation, mutations are properly brand-new plants—and can be christened with new names. So keep an eye on your plants. If you see supposedly plain-colored leaves patterned with yellow or white; a smooth leaf twisted up into a tube; a somber leaf with unexpected brighter color or markings—make sure this is a true mutation, then go ahead. Propagate, christen, and register your new member of the begonia family.

HYBRIDIZING

Far from reserving this fascinating field for themselves, professionals are eager for the amateur's help. And in begonias, even the beginning hybridist has one of the easiest and most exciting chances to succeed. The begonias' constant supply of separate male and female flowers simplifies the procedure immensely. Begonia seeds ripen in about six weeks; new hybrids mature usually within a year. Not many other kinds of plants çan claim such speed. And begonias come in so many sizes, shapes, colors, and forms of closely related plants, the possible combinations are countless and still almost untapped.

Objectives

Hybridizing may be called a "game of chance," but it's wiser not to play it the chancy way. Success comes faster and more surely when you start out with some definite purpose in mind.

Planned parentage naturally aims at lusty, strong, vigorous off-spring. The children of species parents are notoriously blessed with "hybrid vigor," which accomplishes this objective easily. Another general but serious and vital goal is: something truly new and different. Not just a slightly smaller, or larger, or darker-colored form of one or both parents—but a new leaf shape or color; a new combination of colorful leaves, and large, double, or more plenteous flowers; a new growing habit, such as dwarf size or tendency to trail.

Some hybridizers' goals may seem farfetched, but who knows? In Nature's world, the seemingly impossible often comes true. Why not, for example, a yellow-flowered wax begonia—and then a double yellow? When will we see the first blue begonia flowers? Can rexes be bred with double tuberous-type flowers; or large-flowered *tuber-hybrida* with brilliant rex-like foliage? Or fragrant wax begonias with patterned, or tapered, or tiny peltate leaves? The dreamy possibilities are endless.

Selecting Parent Plants

Some general principles are of help to the beginning hybridizer. Obviously it's a waste to repeat someone else's previous cross. And, logically, the more closely related the parents, the easier hybridization becomes. Two rhizomatous begonias, for example, are more likely to mate and produce fertile seeds than a rhizomatous crossed with a tuberous plant.

When two natural species are used as parents, the seedlings from one pod are all closely similar or identical, and inherit similar characteristics from each of the parents. When two hybrids are crossed—or a species is crossed with a hybrid—the seedlings will vary, often to the extent that no two are alike. These have to be grown on to maturity before the outstanding new plants can be selected with accuracy.

Some few hybrids, like 'Ricinifolia,' can be used in hybridizing with fairly predictable results, because their dominant characteristics have become established over a long period of time. When self-pollinated, these will consistently reproduce in their own image.

Dominant characteristics are an important consideration. With begonias which have not been used previously as parents—and there are many—you may have to guess, or hope, that the flower form or leaf shape you want to perpetuate is dominant and will be bestowed liberally on the progeny.

With many begonias, hybridizers' past experience has proved some points. Hybrids of *boweri,* for example (even great-great-great-great grandchildren), usually have leaves blanket-stitched on the edge; *dayi* bequeaths a distinct marking over the main veins; *kenworthyi* contributes a purplish cast to the leaves; the seersucker pucker of the leaves of *acida* is usually transmitted. And *semperflorens* begonias are such forceful parents that, no matter what other type they are crossed with, the result is another, even though slightly different, semp.

You can also profit by others' previous experience in selecting parents which are most likely to be fertile or to set seed. The frequent use of some varieties is a tip-off on their readiness. Begonias *boweri, dichroa, dregei, fuchsioides, heracleifolia, imperialis,* 'Limminghei,' 'Lucerna,' *manicata, mazae, metallica, scharffiana, strigillosa, sunderbruchi,* and 'Viaudi' have been prodigious parents.

Among varieties known to be good seed setters, but not necessarily fertile pollen bearers, are: *odorata rosea, peltata,* 'Pearli,' 'Speculata,' 'Abel Carriere,' and *tomentosa.* Good pollen-bearing producers are: *chimborazo, sanguinea, coccinea, evansiana,* and most rexes. For some strange reason, 'Corbeille de Feu' usually proves to be sterile.

Also strangely, huge, overfertilized plants do not usually set seed readily; nor do weak, undernourished plants. The happy medium of unforced, natural growth is most desirable.

Having decided what type of begonia you hope to create, and having selected healthy, fertile parents which may contribute the desired characteristics, you prepare to pollinate. Now you're off on a fascinating adventure which gets more and more interesting every day and may lead you to the satisfaction of creating something exciting and really new.

How new begonias are born: FIRST ROW TOP: *boweri* crossed with *hydro-cotylifolia* created 'Spaulding.' SECOND ROW: chance seedlings 'Charm' and 'Maphil.' THIRD ROW: *dayi* x *liebmanni*—'Skeezar.' FOURTH ROW: mutations, calla-lily begonia and lettuce-leaved 'Bunchi.'

Pollinating

When your hybridizing has a definite goal, you're not in the market for chance seedlings, which can confuse your calculations no end. So if there's any possibility that insects might beat you to the pollinating, either isolate the mother plant or tie a paper or plastic bag around the flower or stalk you plan to use. Some say, also, that pinching off all flowers you won't use will send more strength to the seed-setting blooms.

It's easy to pick out your parent flowers. The characteristic female begonia blossom has the three-winged ovary below the petals. In its heart grows the yellow pistil, swollen on the end, which receives fertilization and passes it on down to the reproductive organs in the ovary.

The male flower is usually a larger version of the female, without the ovary. In its center, stamens bear soft, dusty golden grains of pollen.

Male begonia flowers often open before the females. If that happens to you, find out first whether the flower has pollen. (It has, if it leaves a deposit of golden dust on the tip of your fingernail when you touch it.) Then, if the selected female flower is not yet open, pick the male and store it in an airtight container in your refrigerator.

When the female flower is open and receptive (the end of the stigma appears shiny and sticky), make your cross. Fold back the petals of the male flower, and dust pollen directly from the stamen onto the stigma of the female. Make the cross both ways—male of Begonia A with female of Begonia B, and vice versa—to give your cross a better chance at success. You can also store the male flower and repeat the pollination every three or four days, until the male is no longer fresh-looking. Experts recommend pollinating between midmorning and midafternoon, in warm air, on a sunny day.

Mark and Record Crosses

Whether or not your cross is successful, it is extremely important to label a fertilized female flower, and to keep complete records on both parents and the results. Tiny jeweler's tags may be tied to the flower stem; or a small sticker gently attached; or a light label stuck on with a bit of cellophane tape. Permanent records of the cross include the parents (female written first), the date, and notes on what happened.

Ripening Seeds

Even the experts have disappointments. A flower may drop without setting seed, or may ripen a pod which contains no seed, or may produce seeds which won't germinate. Reasons vary. Perhaps the parents are too different, or simply incompatible—try others. Perhaps the mother is a poor seed setter—try another, or use the male flowers in a different cross. Either plant may be overforced or starved—select more normal plants.

When a cross does "take," the stigma soon dries and the petals fall. The ovary swells, then dries, and seeds may be harvested. Sometimes the stem will dry up prematurely and drop the seed pod before it is fully ripe. These seeds can usually be ripened by storing in a dry place for a few weeks.

Ripe seeds are dry, brown, dustlike inside the crisp, papery ovary. Before planting them, carefully remove the chaff, which invites mold and rot.

Trial-Testing New Hybrids

Young seedlings which promise to live up to your hopes and expectations must still retain their desirable characteristics when mature, and must be proved propagatable and strong enough to survive in less than ideal environment. Some growers farm the plants out, to be test-grown under varying conditions in different parts of the country. The American Begonia Society also trial-tests new varieties.

Seedlings which show some signs of the desirable characteristics you aimed at—but not to the extent you hoped for—can be crossed with each other and recrossed, or crossed back on the parent, to develop the characteristics more fully. Frequently a good second generation turns up when the first was disappointing.

NAMING NEW BEGONIAS

To repeat a vitally important principle: new varieties, be they mutations, chance seedlings, or hybrids, should not be named, registered, or distributed unless they are truly new, desirably different. This can be established by submitting the new plant to the American Begonia Society, official United States authority on registration of begonias. The plant will be grown and observed, its name checked against prior claim, and its official registered number and description published, to protect the originator.

The new International Code of Nomenclature, formulated within the last few years, contains some sound rules which help avoid confusion and make the selection of names orderly and accurate. A name should not be the same as, or even similar to, a name previously bestowed on another begonia. An unfortunate example is found in the two species, *velloziana* and *vellozoana,* both named for Vellozo, but entirely and confusingly different begonias.

Latin names are reserved for species. Abbreviations like "Mrs." and the articles "a" and "the" are not permissible. Names of living people should not be used without permission; and names of politically prominent people are risky to use at all. (What do you suppose happened to the orchid named 'Stalin'?) Brevity is a virtue; two words are the maximum allowed. Superlatives such as "smallest" or "greatest" should be avoided, because an even smaller or greater variety could conceivably be created later.

Some of the most memorable names are colorfully descriptive— 'Dark Beauty,' 'Silver Jewel.' Naming all your hybrids according to a set scheme—if it is likely that you will create and register more than a few—is a quick way to identify yourself as the hybridizer. The names may all be from mythology—or they may be the names of streets in your town or of members of your family, for example.

Come on, don't miss the fun—or the chance that you might be the proud creator of next year's newest, most exciting begonia. With only two begonias in your window and a goal in mind, you can hybridize!

CHAPTER 18

Exhibiting Begonias

Whether you're a "lone wolf" or a member of a plant-loving group or club, exhibiting your begonias gives you a worth-while reason for growing them. At flower and garden shows—large or small, local or international—you will meet, and share experiences with, other growers and collectors. Not to mention the valuable service you perform for the public (and, of course, for begonias) when you put your prize plants on parade.

Above all, no matter what type of show it is, no matter how unlikely you may think your chances of winning, no matter how busy you are—enter! Don't entertain the mistaken impression that other growers' entries are bound to be better than yours, or you may join the sad ranks of onlookers who whimper about the "better plants [they have] at home." Enter the best plants you can, and as many as you can. Enter at every possible opportunity. At every show, you learn something—about your own plants, or someone else's problems. Experience brings confidence, and confidence leads to success. Keep on entering until you have no more room for your trophies.

HOW TO ENTER A SHOW

For every flower or garden show, there is a schedule of classes—either printed for distribution or available for inspection. Your first step is to get a schedule, or study one. Locate the classes you may want to enter. Make sure you select the correct classes: amateurs do not usually compete with commercial growers; house-grown plants don't vie with greenhouse specimens. If you have any questions, clear them up with some member of the show committee or staff.

Naturally, many shows are general in appeal and are not planned primarily for begonias, or staged by people interested mainly in begonias. So your schedule may not have been designed with begonias particularly in mind. It may not offer as many suitable classes, or competition of the kind you hoped for.

Often, schedule makers are not especially familiar with begonias; they can't possibly know everything about all plants. Get your questions answered early—not when it's too late to make adjustments. If you don't raise the questions, you can't complain about the setup when the show is open.

In addition to classes exclusively for begonias, here are some of the general types of house-plant classes into which begonias usually fit:

> Gardens, mass displays.
> Information booths.
> Collections of plants—a specified number of pots, or a specified space to be filled.
> Plants: flowering, foliage, bulbous and tuberous, hanging basket, window-box.
> Miniature or dish gardens; terrariums.
> Flower compositions; corsages; table settings.

The larger gardens, displays, and booths are usually executed in co-operation with other growers, or by your gardening group or club. The others are usually individual projects. For either type, decide on your entry as early as possible, send in your entry blank, and fulfill all other requirements on time.

GARDENS AND MASS DISPLAYS

Again, in planning large-scale exhibits, the first step is to check and recheck the show schedule. Think about the show's theme, and how your entry can tie in with it. Read all the rules—not once, but twice. Find out all you can about requirements for the class you selected. Should your "message" be educational, or beautiful, or (most effectively) both?

If it's available—and it usually is—check the scale of judging points for the qualities judges will be looking for, and rating you by, when they inspect your entry. For example, garden exhibits are often rated according to a point scale like this:

Judge for yourself—which plant would win first prize? *Dayi* name is misspelled; "strawberry begonia" is entered in wrong class; 'Red Camellia' has too few flowers for semp; 'Marie B. Holley' is lopsided. 'Rufida' is not neatly staked; 'Dancing Girl' loses to 'Helen Lewis' in top row, because it is less rare, less difficult to grow.

Design	25 points
Plant material	25 points
Appropriateness and seasonableness	20 points
Condition of plants	15 points
Labeling of plants	15 points
	100 points

This means that the judges may award you a maximum of 25 points for an excellent design, or a minimum 0 for an impossible one; that your selection of plant material can win you 25 points or less. The winning exhibit is the one which receives the highest total of points.

Next, you need a central idea around which to plan. Perhaps you can illustrate summering begonias out-of-doors, with a lath house or on a patio. Or you may design an old-fashioned begonia garden, or a Gay Nineties parlor bay window—playing up some of the favorite old-time species and hybrids. Or you could demonstrate the wide variety of begonias by grouping specimens of different types together in pyramids, or on stands. For this you would probably need an explanatory chart or sign.

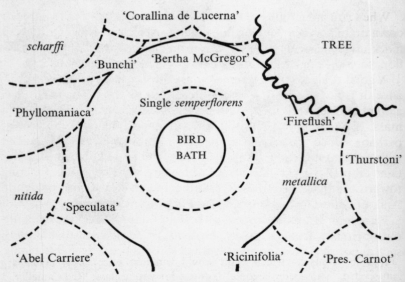

Floor plan for exhibit, "An Old-Fashioned Begonia Garden," could be posted so visitors could identify begonia varieties.

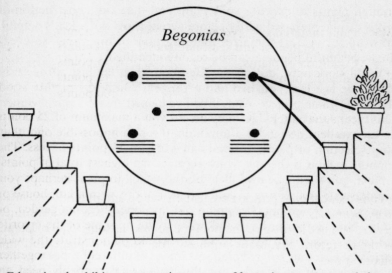

Educational exhibit groups various types of begonias on steps or shelves, with ribbons running to names of groups on chart.

When you are notified of the location of your exhibit, put your idea down on paper as a detailed floor plan or sketch to scale. Or make a mock-up (small-scale replica—easy with cardboard) of any construction, so you can check its design, proportion, and over-all effect.

A good design for a garden or mass display has eye-pleasing balance; it is not overloaded on one side, light on the other. It also has a point of interest or focus; it is not a dull, unaccented, uninteresting mass. If possible, this point of interest should be plant material—perhaps a spectacularly large specimen begonia, or one overloaded with brilliant flowers. Failing this, use something like a bench, fountain, or pool. Tricks like walks which are wide in front, tapering toward the back, give the effect of perspective, distance, or depth. And, of course, colors must be used in effective harmony.

Plan your display to appear as real and natural as possible, without obviously artificial props or effects, or unpleasant distractions, such as pot rims showing above garden soil in a bedded mass of plants.

In any plan, plants should be featured over accessories or elaborate equipment. It is plants that people visit a flower or garden show to see. As a precaution, make sure that you can count on more than enough plants to execute your plan, and that any construction or props can be prepared easily before actual show time. If it's helpful, draw up for visitors a master planting map or diagram—so every single, beautiful begonia can be readily identified.

You'll work hard, but on the Big Day, when the last pot is set in place, the last leaf polished and arranged, you'll feel mighty good about the whole project. And, if you've helped create a prize winner, you'll feel even better.

INFORMATION BOOTHS

These educational projects are usually set up and manned by clubs, or by branches of national plant societies. They are a community service, planned to inspire the public's interest in some type of plant, giving in return favorable publicity for both the plant and the organization.

Again, be sure to check the show schedule for all rules and requirements, and to study the scale of judging points. It may look something like this:

Importance of message	20 points
Clarity of message	20 points
Condition of plants	20 points
Design	20 points
Labeling	20 points
	100 points

Obviously, a plan for an information booth should have an educational theme. One effective idea illustrates the many lands in which begonias are found—featuring a large map of the world or a rotating globe. From the countries of origin, ribbons run to the plants found growing there.

Another good idea is to illustrate the wide variety of begonias and group them according to classes, with an explanatory chart. Or one portion of a booth can demonstrate propagation—how to grow begonias from seed, from stem and rhizome cuttings, from leaves—backed up by specimens of the plants which can be propagated in these fascinating ways.

If possible, get your plan down clearly on paper, so you know ex-

Tabletop educational exhibit shows step-by-step propagating procedures, from seeds and cuttings to mature plants.

Exhibit idea—begonias in a bay window—demonstrates good decorating and cultural principles.

actly what you must produce: how many people, props, and plants you will need; whether or not your message seems likely to come across clearly.

In very large shows, it is usually wise to have a barrier across the front of the booth, so crowds won't push in and trample booth attendants and plants. In any show, someone must be on hand whenever the show is open, to answer visitors' questions. If your group can afford it, quantities of sheets giving brief cultural and other begonia information should be mimeographed or otherwise reproduced, to be handed out. If yours is a branch of the American Begonia Society, the society will supply some helpful material on request.

PLANTS

Whether you are entering a large collection, a few pots, or a single plant—once again, be sure to check the show schedule for all rules, and for tips you can gather from the judging scales. Here are two samples:

CLASS 101—One begonia, *semperflorens*

Flowers	35 points
Cultural perfection	25 points
Foliage	20 points
Rarity	15 points
Labeling	5 points

CLASS 402—Collection of foliage plants, to fill an area 6 ft x 3 ft (Rex begonias qualify here.)

Distinction	30 points
Variety	20 points
Condition	20 points
Labeling	15 points
Color	10 points
Rarity	5 points

Don't underestimate the importance of proper labeling—it can make all the difference between a winning exhibit and second-best. Check reference books, if necessary. Make sure you know your begonias, which class they properly belong in, and how their names are spelled.

PREPARING PLANTS FOR COMPETITION

As soon as you have settled on your entry, select the plants most likely to be in top shape at show time. They need not be rare or difficult varieties, or unusually large. Rather, they should be well-grown and well-groomed specimens according to their type.

Place your promising plants in favored growing locations. If you find that they grow too fast, move them to a cooler place; if they don't develop rapidly enough, give them more warmth—particularly in winter. Watch for danger signs. If leaves look limp, provide better light, cooler temperature, and less water. If leaf color is pale, fertilize. Do everything you can to help your plants develop firm, sturdy foliage and flowers.

Symmetry

There are several ways you can help your plants to grow into compact, well-rounded specimens. Rotate pots on window sills, a quarter-turn each day, so that all sides benefit equally from the light. Some varieties shape up better if they are pinched back, but not immediately before flowering. Some requires staking, with stakes as nearly invisible as possible, never showing above the top of the plant.

Flowers

Semperflorens, angel-wing, and other types grown primarily for their flowers should be in peak bloom on judging day. Judges will weigh both quantity of bloom and quality—size, texture, color. Do not wire flower stems.

Foliage

Carefully remove imperfect stems and leaves; wipe each leaf clean with crumpled, dry tissue paper. For fragile, hairy leaves, use a camel's-hair brush. All foliage should have good color and texture.

Disease or Injury

Examine your plants at the last minute for puckered or stunted leaves or stems; signs of insects or disease; bruise or "mechanical" injury. Diseased or insect-ridden plants may be disbarred; blemished foliage on your plant can give the prize to someone else.

Finishing Touches

Extra points are often won because pots are perfectly clean, and in proper proportion to the size of the plant—usually slightly smaller than the spread of foliage. Soil on top of the pot should be clean, fresh-looking. Accurate, suitable labels should be prepared according to show directions.

SHOW ETIQUETTE AND PLANT CARE

Before bringing in your plants, water them thoroughly. You may also protect them from drying out with a top dressing of damp peat. While your plant is on stage at the show, water it regularly and remove any fallen leaves or flowers.

When you place your plants in their assigned spot, follow all show rules to the letter—and start in plenty of time to finish and quietly vanish when the judging begins. Good sportsmanship will guide you after that.

BIBLIOGRAPHY

Begonia and Shade Plant Show Handbook. Dorothy S. Behrends. Los Angeles, California: Barrow T. Welty, 1953.

The Begonian. Los Angeles, California: American Begonia Society. Monthly publication.

Begonias. Eva K. Gray. Pacific Beach, California: Privately printed, 1931.

Begonias. Bronx, New York: New York Botanical Garden, 1940.

Begonias and How To Grow Them. Bessie R. Buxton. New York, New York: Oxford, 1946.

Begonias for American Homes and Gardens. Helen K. Krauss. New York, New York: Macmillan, 1947.

Buxton Check List of Begonias. Los Angeles, California: American Begonia Society, 1957.

Climate and Man. (*Yearbook of Agriculture*) Washington, D. C.: U. S. Department of Agriculture, 1941.

Exotica II. Alfred Byrd Graf. Rutherford, New Jersey: Julius Roehrs, 1959.

Tuberous Begonias. Worth Brown. New York, New York: Barrows, 1948.

THE AMERICAN BEGONIA SOCIETY

This is a nonprofit organization affiliated with the American Horticultural Society, American Horticultural Council, and the Los Angeles State and County Arboretum, which, since its founding in 1932, has had these aims and purposes: "... to promote interest in begonias and other shade-loving plants; to encourage the introduction and development of new types of these plants; to standardize the nomenclature of begonias; to gather and publish information in regard to kinds, propagation, and culture of begonias and companion plants; to issue a bulletin which will be mailed to all members of the Society; and to bring into friendly contact all who love and grow begonias."

The society maintains research and test gardens, an identification garden, a school of judging, slide library, and speakers' bureau. Membership privileges include borrowing books from the society library, buying seeds of rare begonias and other plants at low cost from the seed fund, sharing views and experience with other members through "round robins."

Annual membership fee is $2.50, which includes a subscription to the monthly bulletin, *The Begonian*. New memberships should be sent to George Schlanert, Membership Secretary, 6525 West 89 Street, Los Angeles 45, California; or sent through any one of the society's branches throughout the country.

WHERE TO BUY BEGONIAS

ANTONELLI BROS., 2545 Capitola Road, Santa Cruz, Calif.—tubers, seeds; mail order.

BARRINGTON GREENHOUSES, 860 Clements Bridge Road, Barrington, N. J.—plants; mail order.

MRS. T. C. BEE, Route 3, Box 120, Newnan, Ga.—plants; mail order.

CARLTON VILLA, 300 Etra Road, Hightstown, N. J.—plants.

FLORENCE CARRELL, 214 North Yale Street, Fullerton, Calif.—seeds.

COUNTRY GREENHOUSES, Cook Hill Road, Danielson, Conn.—plants; mail order.

C. A. CRUICKSHANK, LTD., The Garden Guild, 1015 Mount Pleasant Road, Toronto 12, Ont., Canada—tubers, plants.

DALY'S GREENHOUSES, Nooseneck Road, Coventry, R. I.—plants.

HENRY FIELD SEED & NURSERY CO., Shenandoah, Ia.—plants; mail-order.

FIFTH AVENUE NURSERY, 2510 West Manchester, Inglewood, Calif.—plants.

ELSA FORT, 6123 Cedar Avenue, Merchantville, N. J.—plants.

FUCHSIA LAND NURSERY, 4699 Centinella Boulevard, Los Angeles, Calif.—plants.

GHOSE & CO., Townend, Darjeeling, India—seeds.

GOLDEN BIRD TROPICALS, Route 1, Richfield Road, Yorba Linda, Calif.—plants; mail order.

HARROLD'S, Grants Pass, Ore.—seeds, tubers; mail order.

HAV'ALOOK GARDENS, 10045 W. Grand River, Fowlerville, Mich.—plants; mail order.

CECIL HOUDYSHEL, 1412 Third Street, LaVerne, Calif.—plants.

INTERSTATE NURSERIES, Hamburg, Ia.—tubers; mail order.

MRS. RUTH IVANS, R. D. 1, Pulaski, N. Y.—plants, seeds; mail order.

JENSEN'S GARDENS, 9515 East Flower Avenue, Bellflower, Calif.—plants.

FLORENCE KNOCK, 5833 Second Avenue South, Minneapolis 19, Minn.—seeds; mail order.

KNOTT'S BERRY FARM, Buena Park, Calif.—plants.

LEATHERMAN'S GARDENS, 2637 North Lee Avenue, El Monte, Calif. —plants; mail order.

LOGEE'S GREENHOUSES, 45 North Street, Danielson, Conn.—plants; mail order.

MANHATTAN GARDEN SUPPLY, 305 N. Sepulveda Boulevard, Manhattan Beach, Calif.—plants.

PERCY L. MERRY, 109 Brookside Road, Needham, Mass.—plants.

MERRY GARDENS, Camden, Me.—plants; mail order.

OPPEN'S GREENHOUSES, 433 Auburn Road, Salem, Ore.—plants; mail order.

PALOS VERDES BEGONIA FARM, 4024 Pacific Coast Highway, Walteria, Calif.—plants.

GEORGE W. PARK SEED CO., Greenwood, S. C.—seeds, tubers; mail order.

PEARCE SEED CO., Moorestown, N. J.—plants, seeds; mail order.

RAINBOW NURSERY, 1635 West Florence, Los Angeles 44, Calif.— plants.

JULIUS ROEHRS CO., Rutherford, N. J.—plants; mail order.

MRS. LEO SPENGLER, 15 West Preston Avenue, Orlando, Fla.—plants; mail order.

STEWART'S GREENHOUSES, R. D. 2, Box 491; Tarentum, Pa.—plants.

SUGAR HILL NURSERY, 45 Main Street, Dalton, Mass.—plants.

TOBE'S, St. Catharines, Ont., Canada—plants; mail order.

TROPICAL GARDENS NURSERY, 1510 West Carson, Torrance, Calif.— plants.

TROPICAL PARADISE, 8825 West 79 St., Overland Park, Kansas— plants; mail order.

VALLEY GREENHOUSE, Northwestern Avenue and Thomas Road, Chestnut Hill, Pa.—plants.

VAUGHAN'S SEED CO., 24 Vesey Street, New York 7, N. Y.—seeds, tubers; mail order.

VETTERLE & REINELT, Capitola, Calif.—tubers, seeds; mail order.

THEO. T. WALLSTEN, Route 117, Bolton, Mass.—plants.

WHISTLING HILL, Box 235, Hamburg, N. Y.—plants; mail order.

VIRGINIA I. WITHEE, Hill Farm Road, Conventry Centre, R. I.— plants; mail order.

YOARS HOUSE PLANT NURSERY, Bunker Hill, Ind.—plants; mail order.

RUDOLF ZIESENHENNE, 1130 North Milpas Street, Santa Barbara, Calif.—plants; mail order; rex seeds.

ZUG'S TROPICAL GARDENS, 307 West Gladstone Avenue, San Dimas, Calif.—plants; mail order.

Index

(Numerals in italics indicate illustrations)